The New Social Policy

The New
Social Policy

Michael Cahill

BLACKWELL
Oxford UK & Cambridge USA

First published 1994

Blackwell Publishers
108 Cowley Road
Oxford OX4 1JF
UK

238 Main Street
Cambridge, Massachusetts 02142
USA

British Library Cataloguing in Publication Data

A CIP catalogue record for this book is available from the British Library.

Library of Congress Cataloging-in-Publication Data

A CIP catalogue record for this book is available from the Library of Congress.

ISBNs: 0–631–17861–9 (hbk.); 0–631–17862–7 (pbk.)

Typeset in Palatino on 10/12pt by Photoprint, Torquay, S. Devon.
Printed in Great Britain by T.J. Press Ltd, Padstow

This book is printed on acid-free paper

CONTENTS

LIST OF FIGURES

LIST OF TABLES

ACKNOWLEDGEMENTS

My debts to the numerous authors who have analyzed social change in general and various policy areas in particular are obvious on every page of this book. Particular thanks are due to colleagues in the Department of Community Studies at the University of Brighton who allowed me a sabbatical term in the summer of 1991 to work on this book: in particular to Peter Squires with whom it was first conceived; and to Tony Hadley, Bob Skelton and Valerie Williamson who read and commented upon draft chapters. I am grateful to John Ferris and Paul Wilding for commenting on an early draft and to the anonymous referees who performed the same service. John Ditch and Michael Hill were kind enough to take the time to read the book at a much later stage. Thanks are due to Simon Prosser at Blackwell Publishers who has supported the project since its inception.

Writing a book in a household with toddlers through to teenagers was at times difficult and I am grateful to my mother and aunt for giving me and my computer houseroom on a number of weekends in 1992. Above all, I owe an immense debt to Vanessa who has been a critical reader, indexer, grammarian and constant source of encouragement and the book is dedicated to her.

Grateful acknowledgement is made to the following for permission to reproduce material: Figure 5.1 from Richard Berthoud and Elaine Kempson, *Credit and Debt: the PSI Report*, Policy Studies Institute, 1992; Figure 7.1 from Central Statistical Office, *Social Trends 1993*, 1993; Figure 7.2 from Chris Gratton and Peter Taylor, *Leisure in Britain*, Letchworth: Leisure Publications, 1987; Figure 7.3 from John Roberts, *The Commercial Sector in Leisure*, London: Sports Council/SSRC, 1979;

the 'Far Side' cartoon by Gary Larson that appears on page 47 is reprinted by permission of Chronicle Features, San Francisco, CA, all rights reserved. Table 1.1 from Central Statistical Office, *Social Trends 1993*, 23; Table 2.1 from Tom Forester (ed.), *The Microelectronics Revolution*, Oxford: Blackwell, 1980; Table 2.2 from M. Hepworth and K. Robins, 'Whose information society?', *Media, Culture and Society*, 10, Sage Publications, 1988; Table 3.1 from Central Statistical Office, *Family Expenditure Survey 1990*; Table 4.1 from Phil Goodwin et al (eds.), *Transport; the new realism*, University of Oxford: Transport Studies Unit, 1991; Table 4.2 from Central Statistical Office, *Social Trends*, 19, 1989; Table 4.3 from *The Older Road User*, Department of Transport, 1989, Crown copyright, reproduced with permission of the Controller of Her Majesty's Stationery Office; Table 4.4 from Transport 2000, *Transport and the Pedestrian*, London, 1989; Table 4.5 from Transport and Health Study Group, *Health on the Move*, 1991; Table 5.1 from Margaret Grieco et al, (eds.) *Gender, Transport and Employment*, Avebury, 1989; Table 5.2 from Central Statistical Office, *General Household Survey 1988*; Table 6.1 from *New Earnings Survey 1992*, HMSO, 1992 Crown copyright, reproduced with permission; Table 6.2 from *Some facts about women*, Manchester: Equal Opportunities Commission, 1992; p. 137 contains material from Frank Laczko and Chris Phillipson, *Changing Work and Retirement*, Open University Press, 1991; p. 182 contains material from Alan Durnings, *How much is enough?*, London: Earthscan, 1992.

INTRODUCTION

A glance at the contents page of this book reveals that the subjects dealt with here are new areas for Social Policy. But do we need a new Social Policy? What is new about it? The initial answer is that we live in a new world where traditional patterns of life and work, old certainties and assumptions have all been disrupted. Science and technology are producing impressive breakthroughs in the understanding of nature and new technologies are transforming the patterns of everyday existence. The topics chosen enable us to explore the changes which have occurred in our society in the post-war period, particularly since the early 1970s, and the ramifications for Social Policy.

We can now see the years 1945–75, when the academic subject of Social Policy and Administration emerged, as the period of the 'classic welfare state' (Lowe, 1993). Certain assumptions underlay the thinking on social policy at that time: a commitment to full employment, the mixed economy, the relations between central and local government. Since then the post-war consensus on welfare (and on so much else) has disappeared. There have been numerous accounts of the way in which Thatcherism restructured the politics and policies of the UK, yet this is to take too narrow a view of the changes which have occurred, and accords Thatcherism too great an importance. What has happened to the British economy and society is part of a global pattern of economic and social transformation affecting all the western industrial countries. There has been so much economic and social change in the past two decades that a complete catalogue would now amount to a large volume. Some of the major social changes are detailed in this book, especially as they impinge upon everyday life. Old certainties have vanished in this new world: the dissolution of the Soviet Union means there can be very few people who now believe that Communism will triumph in the battle against the capitalist system. New global problems have appeared: principally the environmental crisis which puts a question mark over the future of the human race.

The chapter headings in this book are Communicating, Viewing, Travelling, Shopping, Working and Playing rather than Health, Personal Social Services, Housing, Education, Employment and Social Security. This does not mean that it is my view that these topics are no longer central to the study of Social Policy. Rather the claim of this book is that we can only provide good social policies if we are sensitive to the context in which government policy programmes operate. Here that context is examined through the perspective of everyday life and each chapter explores the old inequalities which persist and the new inequalities which have been produced. Adopting this perspective does mean that we must see Social Policy as part of a wider public policy: health care is a good example where governments now acknowledge that many other public policies have a health dimension. But the process should work the other way as well: transport policies are dependent on housing and retailing policies, retailing policies have health dimensions and so on. One could produce a long list of these policy inter-dependencies, but the fact remains that they are not acknowledged and acted upon. It should be clear by the end of the book that these new forms of inequalities require a more integrated approach which is beyond the scope of this introductory text.

The academic study of Social Policy and Administration has responded to enormous social and economic changes: studies of un-employment, new forms of poverty, the regional impact of economic decline, the altered status of women and the impact of economic and social disadvantage upon ethnic minorities all attest to this. The economy and society have changed and so too has the field of Social Policy. The Beveridge era ended in the 1970s – the consensus on the shape of the 'welfare state' was weakened by the strains of growing unemployment, finally expiring with the adoption of monetarism by the Conservative government of Mrs Thatcher in 1979. For some years in the 1980s the response of Labour was to defend the public sector while admitting that in some parts it had become over-bureaucratic and alienated some clients and users: now it would appear that the Labour leadership have adopted the language of rights, contracts and consumers. It seems as though the market is now here to stay as an integral part of public service provision, given the substantial adoption of managerialism in the health and social services with the implementation of the NHS and Community Care Act 1990. Indeed, it may well be the case that a new consensus is emerging, with Left and Right committed to both state intervention and the use of markets.

There has been another shift from the public to the private in the social and political life of Britain. This is less remarked upon but is perhaps more important as it has altered our self-identity. The era in which the Beveridge consensus was born – the 1940s – was very different from the present. Then most people used public transport to get to work, a majority of households rented their housing, a minority of them had telephones and for the great majority of the people a television set was just something they had heard discussed on the wireless. All this was to change in the 1950s and 1960s as an era of affluence and consumer goods dawned. In many ways it now seems remarkable that the post-war consensus on welfare survived into the 1970s when the culture out of which it had emerged had long disappeared. The world of the privatized individual needs more extensive exploration than it has received so far and in part this explains the selection of topics in the chapters below, which present an initial exploration of this world.

Information Technology (IT) is the technological development which has made the greatest impact on everyday lives in the last two decades, and this process is explored in chapter 2, Communicating. IT poses challenges to the organisation of society and is transforming work and social life. At the same time IT presents many opportunities which can be utilized to meet social need. Television has assumed a major importance in most of our lives and many household routines and activities have been reorganized to take account of this. Arguably it has been the major influence in the privatization of everyday life. Chapter 3, Viewing, explores the implications for social life. But as well as being a major leisure activity, for most of us viewing is also our window on the world and constitutes a public sphere which is clearly of paramount importance for the discussion of social and public policy issues. Television has supplanted Parliament as the nation's forum for the discussion of day-to-day political issues and political meetings are now sparsely attended. Chapter 4, Travelling, is devoted to the social implications of our transport system and demonstrates the ways in which people's access to transport enables, or inhibits, their participation in a society where personal mobility is taken for granted. Shopping is one of those everyday activities which most of us have to do but which has received little attention from writers on Social Policy. In a complex industrial society shopping is the principal means by which most of us obtain our food and the wherewithal to live our lives. Yet the purchase of goods has become so much more than that: for many it is a form of self-expression which lends meaning to life. This is a perfect illustration of how social life has changed since the Second World War and these themes are explored in chapter 5. For most people work, and the wages it provides, is the entrée to the world of consumerism. In post-war Britain work has become the central form of identity, yet the re-appearance of mass unemployment and the major contraction of manufacturing industry has redrawn the occupational map. These changes are examined in chapter 6, Working. Finally, chapter 7, Playing looks at the importance of leisure, the way in which we spend our leisure and the impact of leisure policies on social inequality.

In the period 1945–75 social democratic thinkers held to the view that the 'welfare state' would combat inequality and create the conditions for a common citizenship or 'welfare society'. The collapse of the post-war consensus on welfare and the emergence of mass unemployment shattered these hopes. Various attempts have been made in the last two decades to pick up the pieces and construct a new understanding of the relationship between the individual and society. The concluding chapter examines three of these perspectives to the extent that they impinge on Social Policy. Lifestyle and consumption have become of central importance in the lives of many millions of people in advanced industrial societies in the post-war period. Retailers increasingly sell us their products by appealing to our search for a different or better identity but the perception of people as primarily consumers or customers has now permeated government and public services. In the final chapter the differing conceptions of political identity are outlined. To pose the question simply: are we consumers or are we citizens?

This book presents a social life analysis of Social Policy. It argues that one cannot understand the changes that are happening to the welfare state – the education service, the health service, the personal social services, housing, the employment services and social security – unless one understands the context in which it operates. There have been many studies of the broader political and economic context of capitalist societies within which welfare states function. The approach of this book is to study the changes that are occurring in the wider world through an examination of social life – the daily ways in

which all of us organize our lives: the work that we do, the food and
clothes that we buy, our entertainment, the way we communicate,
the programmes we watch on television – and to demonstrate how
inequalities and divisions are manifest in these areas and how,
indeed, new ones are being created. Social policy needs to be in touch
with the ordinary concerns of people as they live their everyday lives
and from this perspective the subjects chosen in this book should
require no further justification.

This then is the context in which we need to view the development
of social services and health services and the other sectors of the
welfare state. What is attempted here is a view of the social services in
which the main areas of welfare provision are explored but from a
different angle. Centre stage are the components of social life while
welfare state services are in the background. Familiar names make
their appearance but sometimes in unfamiliar roles: W H Beveridge,
for instance, but as author of his 1951 report on broadcasting rather
than as author of the report on Social Insurance. The intention is to
put the welfare state in its place, which is not, as we are all surely
aware, at centre stage. Although social policy analysts might regret
the fact, it is still nonetheless the case that the great majority of people
in this country are seldom interested in the social policy measures of a
government. The queues in High Holborn for the publication of the
Beveridge Report in 1942 were exceptional and occurred more than
fifty years ago.

This does not mean that people are uninterested in the products of
government. The decision which means that the bus service to the
village no longer runs, the plan to move the inner city hospital to the
outskirts of the town, the move to close the local swimming baths in
order to pay for a brand new leisure centre only really accessible to
motorists, are all questions of access. Access needs to become a key
term in the vocabulary of social policy for it is important for so many
of the users of services; older people, disabled people, children. As
we will see in the book, the dimensions of poverty and inequality can
be carried through into the analysis of social life: the information-rich
and the information-poor, the employment-rich and the employment-
poor, the transport-rich and the transport-poor and so on.

There are many precedents for taking an extended view of Social
Policy. Social investigators a hundred years ago took a broader view
of the human condition than most contemporary social policy
analysts. Charles Booth is celebrated for his pioneering work on
poverty but he wanted to go down in history for his many volumes
on the religious behaviour of the London poor. Similarly, Seebohm

Rowntree's interests were far more wide ranging than the investigation of poverty in York, and he produced a book on leisure long before it became a respectable area of academic investigation (Rowntree and Lavers, 1951). But Booth and Rowntree were not academics. They wrote before the issues of poverty, bad housing, unemployment and health care had been colonized by numerous specialists working in the universities and before the bifurcation of Sociology and Social Administration had taken root.

Richard Titmuss, acknowledged to be the major force behind the creation of the subject area of Social Policy and Administration, took a wide-angle perspective on the issues of social change and welfare, drawing on the resources of social history, sociology, social anthropology and economics. Almost forty years ago in 1955 Titmuss demonstrated the existence of a fiscal welfare system, that of tax allowances operated by the Inland Revenue; and an occupational welfare system, that of company cars, occupational pensions and other benefits which accrue to individuals from employment. Titmuss insisted that these systems had to be set alongside the social services and that together they constituted the social division of welfare. Adrian Sinfield extended this analysis to highlight the importance of the relationship between government and business in the provision of welfare and, more suggestively, to point to the significance of time as a resource: 'the differential ability of individuals, families, classes and organisations to plan or make arrangements over time' for their welfare (1978, p. 149). The Titmuss approach was amended by Hilary Rose to encompass the family and the home: in particular looking at who does the domestic labour and caring. This is what Rose refers to as the sexual division of welfare. Rose puts a welcome emphasis on the micro in contrast to the political economy of the late 1970s which situated welfare state services within the context of class and power and economic life (1981). The chapters of this book may be said to explore the micro for they are concerned with the daily tasks of shopping, working and travelling as well as the daily pleasures of watching television and other leisure pursuits. The focus is on the theme of inequality in the examination of social change and social life. Although some feminist social policy writers have highlighted the importance of issues of transport and access in relation to health and community care this has not been generally acknowledged in the literature (Land, 1989).

Transport has become increasingly important as a generator of inequalities as the public provision of transport has declined. It is a classic example of the diswelfares produced by the operation of a market system in which certain individual choices have been guided and formed by powerful economic interests — motor car manufacturers, oil companies, the road haulage industry – while others have been ignored and marginalized. Transport is also a good illustration of the inter-dependencies of modern society: seen most clearly each day in many parts of the country when traffic tails back for many miles, and with the pollution created by motor vehicles. Titmuss highlighted the inter-dependencies of modern society, but now we can see more clearly than in the Titmuss era how the organization of social life is important for the welfare of individuals and groups. Any definition of welfare restricted to 'welfare state' services is an impoverished one: most people gain their sense of well-being in large part from social life. It is quickly clear from any study of the major forms of social life that the prosperous and the powerful can utilize their position to maximize their welfare. The social changes described in chapter 1 and the emerging political consensus on markets and the state have put the self-maximizing individual at centre stage. But this can mean that the weak, members of minorities, the poor and others will see their position and interests deteriorate in this new world. How to prevent this occurring must be one of the central tasks for Social Policy in the 1990s.

References

Land, H (1989) in M Bulmer, et al. (eds), *The Goals of Social Policy*, London: Unwin Hyman.

Lowe, Rodney (1993), *The Welfare State in Britain since 1945*, London: Macmillan.

Robson, W A (1976), *Welfare State and Welfare Society*, London: George Allen and Unwin.

Rose, Hilary (1981), 'Rereading Titmuss: the sexual division of welfare', *Journal of Social Policy*, 10, 4, 477–502.

Rowntree, B Seebohm and Lavers, G R (1951), *English Life and Leisure: a social study*, London: Longman, Green and Co.

Sinfield, A (1978), 'Analyses in the Social Division of Welfare', *Journal of Social Policy*, 7, 2, 129–56.

Titmuss, R M (1958), *Essays on 'The Welfare State'*, London: Allen and Unwin.

1

SOCIAL POLICY AND SOCIAL CHANGE

This chapter provides a brief outline of social change in post-war Britain. The pace of change – economic, social and technological – is so great that it is said that we are moving into a new era. One early characterisation of this in the 1970s was the term 'information society' which denoted a society in which information had replaced capital as the key resource (see chapter 2). Although there are many critics of this theory it is undeniable that the impact of information technology in the past twenty years has been enormous. Micro electronics, the routine and widespread application of computer technology, has revolutionized the manufacture and distribution of goods and services. Perhaps most important for all of our lives are the employment consequences with millions of workers, particularly the low skilled or unskilled, thrown out of work in the western economies. In this process the UK has been disproportionately hit because of the age of its manufacturing base. Total employment in manufacturing had been declining since the 1960s and fell particularly sharply in the first half of the 1980s. Information technology has also produced many benefits: with the enhanced access to information which computers provide, some workers have seen their horizons and opportunities expand. Companies have been able to utilize information technology to increase greatly the data available to them about their performance.

The linkage between telecommunications and information technology has meant the ability to transfer information across the globe, and the arrival of fibre optic links heralds an age in which information will be capable of transfer via the medium of voice, image or text on an almost limitless scale. These developments have made the world smaller. Time and space have been compressed: the reduction in travel times has meant that distances are reduced and this process has accelerated in the last two decades. Facsimile machines (faxes) and modems ensure that printed information can be sent across the world within minutes. International travel has reduced distances dramatically so that it is possible to conduct meetings with participants from across the world much more easily.

Globalization is an important feature of the late twentieth century and can be seen in a variety of contexts. In the mass media satellite technology enables programmes to be beamed into a country from all over the world. Cultural products, such as films or videos, can now be made for a world market: 'world music' is a recent phenomenon. Satellite TV removes national boundaries in television. Programmes can be beamed to all the countries of Western Europe or all those in the Far East. Not only do people want to see programmes from all over the world but they want to see the world for themselves, and this has led to a big expansion in the amount of recreational travel. Tourism is now the world's largest industry. Sometimes the worlds of tourism and entertainment are inter-linked as with the annual pilgrimages of people from all over the globe to Disneyworld.

Economic globalization has meant that there is now a world market in many industries with production being organized on a global basis: a product can be assembled in one country after its components have been manufactured in another. Most major companies compete in a world market. The process of the amalgamation of economic enterprises has continued apace, with multinational corporations becoming even larger and more powerful. The European Community, which started out as an economic trade area, has now spawned numerous initatives in Social Policy and encouraged inter-European cooperation among countless groups and associations. The process of Europeanization became more marked with the creation of the Single Market in 1992, in which workers and businesses have the potential to move freely among the member states of the European Community. This too is part of a process of globalization in which national frontiers matter less and the world seems to become smaller as horizons are widened.

The economic system of production which dominated the western world from the end of the Second World War until the mid 1970s was mass production for a mass market. This has been characterized as Fordism, because it was pioneered by Henry Ford, who organized production on a conveyor belt process so that each worker did the same task over and over again. The resulting economies enabled Ford to cut the price of his cars dramatically and hence appeal to a mass market. The products of the post-war consumer society were manufactured in this way – the fridges, cars, televisions, record players, tape recorders, radios – and the producive process was organized in such a way that each worker had only a small part to play in the productive process, mechanically repeating the same small task. Since the mid 1970s there would seem to have been two developments which indicate a new phase in economic production, usually known as 'Post-Fordism'. The internationalization of production made possible by information technology allows firms to divide parts of the production process between plants in different countries. Flexible specialization is the production of short runs of customized goods for a 'niche' market. Again, computers enable this to occur as each stage of the production process is integrated into a single coordinated system. This is characterized by short runs of different products which are produced for smaller 'niche' markets, in which consumers want a particular product to be different in design and style from others. Nowadays manufacturers will appeal to niche markets which in one country will be much smaller than the mass market but across the globe will often be quite substantial. Post-Fordism is a response to a consumer market in which identity, difference and diversity have become all-important. Marketing has become an extremely important part of the world of business and manufacturing. Manufacturers and retailers need to be aware of the tastes, aspirations and goals of individuals in order to tailor their products to meet these desires. Marketing has become an industry in its own right with thousands of people employed in market research attempting to assess our reactions to innumerable products.

The extent to which our processes of production, distribution and exchange are Post-Fordist or in some areas still Fordist is a matter of some debate. Rationalization has been an important part of the success of Fordism in the manufacture of products and this is being applied to service industries. McDonald's restaurants are an example of a Fordist approach to the manufacture and selling of hamburgers. The McDonald's company has taken rationalization to new heights for service industries. The problem with selling hamburgers used to be getting the same consistent product, given the large number of variables involved in the process. Human beings differ greatly in their abilities, aptitudes and experience in the cooking of hamburgers. The success of McDonald's lies in large part in being able to ensure that wherever you are in the world the product will taste the same. This is achieved by rationalizing all the processes to the extent that there is very little opportunity for human error. The same company works to ensure a very high throughput of customers at their stores by making the seats sufficiently uncomfortable that twenty minutes is about the most our bottoms can take. There is a real sense in which this process of rationalization can be said to have spread to other products and services (Ritzer, 1993). The selling of food via out-of-town superstores puts a great deal of the work onto the customer – the driving to the store, the selection of the goods, the packing of the goods – all of which would in the past be done by staff who would have had to be paid.

The Decline of Britain

Although there has been considerable social change in Britain since 1945 there has been little political change. Political institutions have the same format as in 1945, with some minor changes such as the occasional use of the referendum and a system of Select Committees in the House of Commons and a reformed system of local government. Centralization of political power has been a marked trend in the last forty years: the balance of power between the centre and the locality has shifted to the former with local government having lost many of its key powers at the instigation of a strong central government, to the extent that central government is now responsible for the major part of local government expenditure.

The global trends have impinged upon a society which has over the last forty years undergone a substantial diminution of its role and status in the world. The UK at the close of the Second World War was a super power which had in concert with the United States and the Soviet Union defeated the Axis powers. But in the process of winning the war the country had bankrupted itself and could only recover to the extent that it did in the post-war period with the assistance of a great deal of American money. The Labour Government of Clement Attlee began the process of decolonization with the granting of independence to India in 1947 and over the next two decades most of the British Empire was granted its independence. This was a successful endeavour in that the new countries in Africa and the Far

East were granted their independence without for the most part any great loss of blood. But Britain was not to find it easy to adapt to a new role as a European country. The UK has declined relative to other European Community states. Its economy has not kept pace with that of its competitors in Europe such as France and Germany.

There is now a considerable literature exploring the multi-faceted nature of the decline of Britain. Within this some key positions can be highlighted. From the New Right, Correlli Barnett has argued that the British made a strategic error in investing so heavily in the new institutions of the welfare state in the 1940s, when they should instead have used what little resources they had left at the close of the war to modernize and re-equip British manufacturing industry. Barnett's 'villains' are those administrators and politicians, like Attlee and Beveridge, who believed that the welfare state should be a priority for post-war Britain. This was to deny the country the chance to compete successfully with other Western European countries. Instead there should have been a substantial programme of investment in industrial production in order to modernize the industrial base (Barnett, 1986). It must be said that the evidence on post-war social security spending does not support Barnett's case: those Western European countries with the highest levels of economic growth had the highest spending on social security (Harris, 1991).

Martin Wiener dates the uncompetitiveness or British industry to the late nineteenth century and blames the anti-industrial attitudes of the governing classes (1981). The pioneering industrialists whose combined efforts produced the 'take off' into industrialization did not form a separate class but were absorbed through the generations into the existing ruling class through a process of gentrification, whereby they bought landed estates and educated their children at public schools. Here the prevailing view was that trade and industry were inferior pursuits to the City of London and the professions.

The Wiener analysis is similar in some respects to that of neo-Marxists who believe that political institutions are outmoded and need dramatic overhaul and reform. There has been far too little investment in manufacturing industry because of the predominant role that the City of London takes in investment decisions, which has meant that it concentrates on gaining maximum returns in the short term and therefore eschews the chance to invest in British industry when returns are so much higher elsewhere in the world economy. Neo-Marxists also trace the decline of Britain back to the late nineteenth century as it was during this period that British industry first became uncompetitive in comparison with other leading industrial countries (Gamble, 1990).

From the centre of the political spectrum David Marquand has essayed one of the most acute and penetrating contributions to our understanding of the decline of Britain. He sees the failure to keep pace with other countries as part of a problem of 'maladaptation' on the part of business, unions and government to the twentieth-century environment. But this is part of a wider malaise which consists of a lack of trust between government and the governed, a pervasive 'possessive individualism' in which sectional interests are promoted at the expense of the public interest and a resort to manipulation rather than persuasion by governments in their efforts to change society (Marquand, 1988, pp. 211–12). The decline of Britain is one of the most disputed and difficult questions in contemporary history and only the major features of this debate have been sketched here. Even so the topic of social change should not be separated from the context of an island in relative decline, off the mainland of Europe.

Although the economy has been outperformed by western competitors it has produced a great deal of prosperity for the population so that there is now a higher GDP per capita than there was in the early 1950s (Halsey, 1987). Shorter hours of work and longer holidays have accompanied the economic growth seen since the 1940s. There have been major changes in the organization of work. There has been a sharp decline in the number of manual workers in the country and this of course has had significant impact on the class structure. In 1951 70 per cent of the workforce were in manual occupations, but by 1981 this figure had declined to 52 per cent (Halsey, 1987). Part time jobs multiplied so that by 1991 they constituted one quarter of the workforce (Hewitt, 1993, p. 14). This is related to the other major trend – the big increase in the number of women in paid employment. The North–South divide was a much remarked upon feature of the 1980s: the concentration of nineteenth-century manufacturing in the North of England and in certain parts of Northern Ireland, Scotland and Wales has meant that these regions were badly affected by the closure of the old, uncompetitive plants in their areas. The increase in the service sector took place not in the North of England but in East Anglia and the South of England (Northcott, 1991, p. 162). The expansion in business services, research and development, finance, advertising and market research was in the South and in East Anglia (McDowell, in Ball et al., 1989, p. 164).

The major population movement has been out of cities towards the suburbs and now increasingly to the countryside. The British are a people possessed by the dream of country life as being superior to an urban existence, or if not the 'good life' then at least an improved

Figure 1.1 Predicted % change in population in England over next 20 years

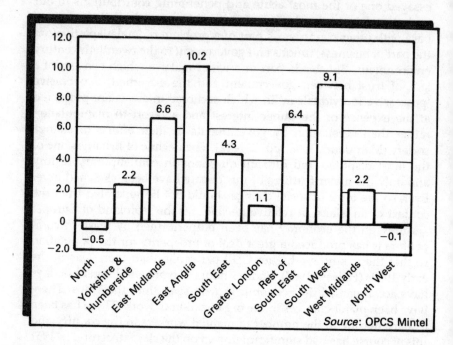

Source: OPCS Mintel

quality of life. Many small towns greatly increased their populations in the 1980s while the older urban areas recorded a net decrease in population. Among them Liverpool's population declined by 8.2%, the central area of Manchester by 9.9% and Salford's by 7.9% (OPCS, 1992). It is claimed on the basis of opinion surveys that more than thirteen million people living in cities want to move to small towns or countryside (figure 1.1).

This movement of people away from the cities has become much more pronounced in the last twenty years corresponding with the much greater availability of motor cars. The result has been a dispersal of population and more problematically a dispersal of facilities such as schools, hospitals and shopping centres, which makes the ownership of a car even more desirable and the penalties for non-ownership more severe in terms of lost opportunities. There are now substantial areas of land in the inner cities which are vacant whilst there are insistent pressures on local authorities to release land for building in the green belts. Inner cities have been the site for serious social unrest: their combination of high unemployment rates, poor housing and often poor local authority services has produced a volatile mixture.

The Decline of the Family

Many social scientists would disagree with this heading. Their response to the statistics which show a decline in two parent families and a rise in one parent families would be to argue that the family is as popular as ever but that it has many different forms to the two parent nuclear family. The debate on the family quickly becomes heated as it relates to personal life and choices so directly. It is distinguished by the paradox of the Right arguing for the importance of a collective form, the family, while the Left largely subscribes to the view that the family should be seen as a group of individuals and it is best to provide for each one separately. There have been numerous changes in the family form in the last two decades consequent upon the Divorce Law Reform Act of 1969 and the challenge to gender roles which has come from the rise of feminism. The highly charged arguments revolve around the significance of statistics on marriage and the family. Between 1961 and 1985 the divorce rate increased fivefold and remarriages now account for more than a third of all marriages. Lone parent families as a percentage of families with dependent children more than doubled in the period 1971 to 1991. Among European Community countries only Denmark has a higher divorce rate as can be seen from table 1.1.

What the results of these changes are for children and for society as a whole are endlessly debated and perhaps the answer will only become apparent in the future. For the present the evidence of the National Child Development Survey, a longitudinal study of a cohort of children born in 1958, shows that children whose parents divorce tend to experience downward social mobility with the result that they are more likely to leave school early, less likely to go into further education and more likely to be in an unskilled job in their early twenties. Housing status tends to be lowered. The effects are worse for children where the parent remarries thus forming a step-family (Family Policy Studies Centre, 1991). For those people who believe that fathers are important for a child's identity and maturation the figures are equally depressing. Within two years of a divorce more than one third of children have lost contact with the non-custodial parent: after ten years more than one half have lost contact altogether

Table 1.1 Marriage and divorce: EC comparison, 1981 and 1990

	Marriage per 1,000 eligible population		Divorces per 1,000 existing marriages	
	1981	1990	1981	1990
United Kingdom[a]	7.1	6.8	11.9	12.6
Belgium	6.5	6.5	6.1	8.7
Denmark	5.0	6.1	12.1	12.8
France[b]	5.8	5.1	6.8	8.4
Germany (Fed. Rep.)	5.8	6.6	7.2	8.1
Greece	7.3	5.8	2.5	–
Irish Republic	6.0	5.0	0.0	0.0
Italy	5.6	5.4	0.9	2.9
Luxemburg[b]	5.5	6.1	5.9	10.0
Netherlands	6.0	6.4	8.3	8.1
Portugal	7.7	7.3	2.8	–
Spain	5.4	5.5	1.1	–
Eur 12	6.0	6.0	–	–

Source: *Social Trends*, 1993, 23.
[a] 1990 column for marriages contains 1989 data and divorce column contains 1987 data.
[b] 1990 column for divorces contains 1989 data.

(Coote et al., 1990). The National Child Development Survey and other longitudinal studies where the effects of parental divorce can be studied demonstrate that contrary to the popular belief held in the 1960s when the divorce laws were liberalized the effects on children of divorce are long lasting and extend into adulthood, where children of divorced parents are more likely to report a higher incidence of depression (Family Policy Studies Centre, 1991).

It is indisputable that social attitudes towards sexuality have changed markedly in the last thirty years. Sex between adult males was decriminalized in 1967 and subsequently there has been an assertion of gay and lesbian identities. The 1960s saw the beginning of a new approach to sexuality and marriage presaging greater freedoms for women. The invention of the contraceptive pill, which gave women the ability to control their own reproduction, can now be seen as a major turning point for in removing the fear of unwanted pregnancy it led to a rise in pre-marital sex and more liberal attitudes to sex outside marriage. The ability of women to control the number and spacing of births improved their ability to plan their lives.

These changes occurred in the 1960s but it was not until the 1970s that feminism, which had its stimulus in the women's liberation movement of the late 1960s, began to be taken seriously by the media and other channels of communication in society. Feminism in its first wave influenced the passage of the Equal Pay Act of 1970 and the Sex Discrimination Act of 1975, but it was also about trying to change social attitudes. Here the evidence seems to indicate that twenty years of feminist pressure has had some impact upon private lives. Gershuny's work, using the evidence of time diaries, shows that in households with full time employed women, those with part time employed women and those with unemployed women, the proportion of housework that men perform increased between 1974 and 1987 (Gershuny, in Abercrombie and Warde, 1992). However, it would appear from what evidence there is available on the household tasks performed by men and women that women still perform the great majority.

The Decline of Class

The theme of class is more hotly contested than most aspects of social change in contemporary Britain. What are not in dispute are the findings that the number of skilled workers has fallen steeply, the numbers of people in professional groups has risen dramatically and the broader point that the middle class – or service class – has increased its number significantly. Over the past twenty years there has been a sharp and irreversible decline in the manufacturing sector of the British economy (Ball et al., 1989, chapter 14).

There has been a further decline in the traditional core of the industrial working class. Old nineteenth-century industries such as ship building, iron and steel production, textiles and mining have suffered an irreversible decline in the face of foreign competition. Newer twentieth-century industries such as motor car manufacture have suffered from foreign competition and the motor car industry in this country is now almost entirely in the hands of foreign companies. The net result of this has been an exacerbation of the North–South divide which emerged in this country in the 1930s, with whole areas becoming depressed because of the loss of their major industries. The impact on the occupational structure of the UK has been marked. The number of employees in the manufacturing sector fell by over forty per cent between 1971 and 1992. In 1992 only one fifth of employees were employed in manufacturing while nearly three quarters were in services (*Social Trends*, 1993, p. 57). It is too strong a claim to say that we are witnessing the 'end of class' as a source of stratification, and it is more accurate to posit a decline of class especially as a source of identity.

Within the years of the post-war consensus on welfare 1945–75 there was a stable two party voting system which reflected a class based voting pattern. Roughly speaking two thirds of the working class electorate voted Labour while two thirds of the middle class voters chose the Conservative Party. Since 1970 a process of class dealignment has taken place in the sense that fewer middle class voters have supported the Conservative Party and fewer working class people have voted Labour. The results for the Labour Party have been discouraging as it would appear that their traditional base in the working class is being eroded. Why this should be so is clearly a complex problem in the study of electoral behaviour. One suggestive analysis has come from Patrick Dunleavy. In contrast to traditional forms of class identity Dunleavy has drawn attention to the 'consumption' location of individuals. His argument is that there are sectoral divides in British society which override occupational group loyalties and attachments. Housing and transport are the two key consumption locations and the crucial distinction is between private and public in both: with the owner occupier and private motorist being swayed in their voting intention by the fact that the Conservative Party is the party seen to best represent their consumption interests (1980; Dunleavy and Husbands, 1985).

Class is important in the distribution of life chances. Clearly social class matters in relation to education, health and housing and many people are aware of the differential advantages enjoyed by people from different class locations. But it is social class as an organizing principle, as a unifying concept which is in sharp decline.

The Rise of Lifestyle

The decline of class as a significant variable in the world of British politics reflects its reduced importance in the perceptions of ordinary people. This is why it is much more difficult for the Labour party to win supporters and why it has begun to redefine its appeal, away from traditional calls for class solidarity towards appeals based on individual self-interest. The inequalities of housing, education and health are now more likely to be seen as being capable of remedy by individuals doing something about it themselves. If they cannot, for example because they cannot afford private health care insurance, then they will support the collectivist solution, the NHS, but because it enables them as individuals to benefit not because they support it as a collectivist enterprise per se. There is equally a high level of support for the private sector (Taylor Gooby, 1991, p. 114).

It is one of the accepted realities of the world of marketing that social class no longer plays the dominant role in individual self-identity which it once did. The different classes are no longer distinguishable to the same extent by the clothes that they wear: greater informality of dress has meant that a variety of styles are open to individuals so that their clothes are no longer the badge of their class. Social class has ceased to be the major determinant on the way that people vote: yes, it is still important but not in the way in which it once was. Market researchers identify a range of status groups within the population which represent the aspirations of people. In the 1980s a social class categorization of the population seemed to be less useful than previously, for there emerged significant differences within the social class categories which reflected both different age groups and different aspirations of the population. The generic term for this is lifestyle, which appears to be straight out of the world of the Sunday colour supplements but has in fact a sociological definition. Bocock defines it as 'individuality, self-expression and a stylistic self-consciousness' (Bocock and Thompson, 1992, p. 138). Housing is a good example of the way in which lifestyle impinges upon social policy – for one of the key aspects of the innumerable lifestyle features which adorn the Sunday supplements are articles on what to do with the decor, furnishing and layout of the home.

The sale of council houses to their tenants – what the Conservative government called 'the right to buy' – may be taken to be symbolic of the way in which the welfare state was forced to respond to the changed aspirations of the population. Many people in council housing wanted to buy their own houses and many councils were agreeable to their sale, but this was not the view of some local authorities who, for very good reasons, wished to keep property which they could allocate on the basis of social need; for other councils it was a point of principle not to sell housing that was collectively owned. There was then a conflict of principle here between the individuals wanting to purchase their homes for all the various reasons that people want to do so – a capital asset, more control over the property – and councils wishing to protect the integrity of their housing stock. The Conservative government of the 1980s with its housing legislation ensured that tenants had the right to buy and because of the subsidies offered actually encouraged them to do so. As so many commentators have pointed out, council housing has now become a residual sector of the housing market for those who cannot gain accommodation elsewhere. The collectivist hope of the past that all classes of people would live in local authority rented accommodation is now buried. Individual choice has been the guiding principle here. In the case of council housing there has been a great deal of official encouragement for people to choose the individual option, although the extent to which many people needed encouragement is open to doubt as many people value the security which they feel home ownership gives them (Saunders, 1990). In other sectors, like transport, there has been no need for official encouragement, for the personal advantages which the car brings to an individual's life – mobility, independence – are real enough. Government's role here has been to manage the resulting decline of public transport. The consumer society encouraged an interest in personal identity – how one looked and dressed became a personal statement or should become one. This particular discourse has not been confined to the marketing men or advertising agencies. The feminist movement, while initially reacting against the advertising copy which suggested a woman's quality of life would improve if she used a different shampoo or washing powder or floor cleaner, came to emphasize the importance of individual identity for women as expressed in assertiveness or equal opportunities. Similarly the Labour Party which once embodied a belief that socialism was about the creation of neighbourliness and community has come to accept the need to appeal to the electorate in terms of individual self-interest. This cultural change came to be seen in transport – you are able to express your personality by the car you buy, how you drive it and so forth. The same personal statements can be made with private housing in a way that one cannot with public housing.

The economic system of consumer capitalism has encouraged the diversity and divergence of style because it provides lucrative markets. Social movements encourage a concentration on self-expression because the 'personal is political' and feminist, gay and lesbian groups wish to see a renegotiation of the bases of everyday life with greater scope for tolerance of unconventional ways of life. Self-expression also helps to make their cause known. The commercial and the social come together in the tee-shirt which has become the billboard for a thousand slogans. Or the mug, the poster, the car sticker. Never before have there been so many ways of proclaiming one's identification with a cause to one's fellow human beings. But one is bound to ask: is anyone listening? Not because they are uninterested but more because there are so many messages to attend to, so many slogans, so many commercials. There has been a fragmentation of the big corporations which enables a diversity of forms to emerge, many of them just at the local level. Take radio. For twenty years after the Second World War there were three national radio services all controlled by the BBC. 1967 saw the launch of a fourth, in the shape of Radio One, and around the same time local BBC stations started to broadcast. In the early 1970s these were supplemented by local commercial stations and now there are national commercial stations and a mix of local stations. This diversity certainly produces a richness of choice but it may be said to make the task of communicating more difficult as there is so much going on. Ethnic minority communities have their own radio stations and the technology is available to enable innumerable new radio stations to broadcast. It is one of the benefits of the new culture of diversity and decentralization that minorities can enjoy their own channels of communication. The national controlled channels still exist but they are supplemented by the local and the particular. There are obvious parallels here with the decentralization which has occurred in economic production. The BBC was a large monopoly public corporation but it could not respond to all the various needs of the population, in part because the number of wavelengths was strictly controlled by international agreement.

This world of diversity and choice has now been introduced into the heartlands of the welfare state, the health service and the personal social services. The NHS and Community Care Act of 1990 introduced the local (quasi) market into the provision of health and social services. Local management of schools is another major step in the creation of a diverse system of administration of schools, although the National Curriculum does ensure some centralized control. Social policy has now become part of the trend towards locally managed and controlled services within a national framework.

The Quality of Life

In both the health service and the social services there is now increasing recognition that income, employment and location play an important part in the health and well-being of the person, although this is not reflected in the government's White Paper *The Health of the Nation*, which sets targets for the personal health of the UK population. Social Services Departments might be persuaded by the accent on user-led services to listen to those disabled and older people who argue that community care involves adequate transport services as well as personal services.

There is no doubt that the new world we now live in – characterized by globalism, decentralization, mobility and diversity – is potentially exciting and presents a range of opportunities, but the forms of inequality produced by class and wealth need to be documented to set alongside this. This book is organized on the basis that the traditional concerns of Social Policy and Administration need to be brought to bear on this new world. There is a real danger that as we delight in the vistas of information and knowledge opened up by microelectronics we will forget the plight of those who cannot read in our society. Or as we linger over the choice of innumerable yoghourts, pastas, delicacies and cheeses at the out of town superstore we forget that many people simply cannot reach these stores as they do not own a car, or that they cannot afford to buy these products as they live on social security.

It is sobering to remember in the context of the opportunities which are undeniably presented by the sophistication of modern technologies and their growing applicability to daily living how many people are largely excluded from their benefits because of the structural changes which have occurred in western industrial economies. Because of changes in social security regulations the economic position of unemployed people worsened in the 1980s. The living standards of the poor as a whole declined in relation to average income (Hills et al., 1990, p. 333).

Numerous studies have documented the impact that life on social security has on families: the reduction of opportunities to participate in society, the restricted options for children, the constant need to be vigilant about expenditure. Understandably some people on benefit do not have the necessary resources of personality to be able to meet this daily challenge and this sometimes results in child neglect and worse. There is a growing fear that Britain is seeing the growth of an 'underclass', 'characterised by drugs, casual violence, petty crime, illegitimate children, homelessness, work avoidance and contempt for conventional values', cut off from the rest of society by physical location – in inner city areas or sink council estates – and excluded from participation in the wider society by low income (Murray, 1990). Whether one accepts the term 'underclass' or not there is an understandable fear that the benefits of contemporary life – its choice, opportunities and freedoms – mediated through the market will be denied to a substantial section of the population. The marketization of so many goods and services is occurring in a society where high rates of unemployment are once more the norm and where alternatives to the value system of consumer capitalism – the labour movement, class and community – have been seriously eroded. This book is in part an examination of those who are excluded from contemporary consumerism.

The six areas of social life introduced in the chapters which follow are not part of the conventional welfare state services and do not feature in other Social Policy texts. Yet they all influence the welfare of individuals and groups, sometimes in quite major ways, and constitute from time to time matters of pressing concern to many people.

Further Reading

Michael Ball et al., in *The Transformation of Britain* (Fontana, 1989) examine the social and economic structure and the extent to which change has occurred. Martin Jacques and Stuart Hall (eds), *New Times* (Lawrence and Wishart, 1989) is a stimulating account of Post-Fordism and globalization and its implications for the polity, economy and society, but principally addressed to the rethinking necessary on the Left.

References

Abercrombie, N and Warde, A (1992), *Social Change in Contemporary Britain*, Cambridge: Polity Press.

Ball, M et al. (eds) (1989), *The Transformation of Britain*, London: Fontana Press.

Barnett, C (1986), *The Audit of War*, London: Macmillan.

Bocock, R and Thompson, K (eds) (1992), *Social and Cultural Forms of Modernity*, Cambridge: Polity Press.

Central Statistical Office (1993), *Social Trends*, London: HMSO.

Coote, A et al. (1990), *The Family Way*, London: Institute of Public Policy Research.

Dunleavy, P (1980), *Urban Political Analysis*, London: Macmillan.

Dunleavy, P and Husbands, C (1985), *British Democracy at the Crossroads*, London: Allen and Unwin.

Family Policy Studies Centre (1991), *Family Policy Bulletin*, December.

Gamble, A (1990), *Britain in Decline*, 3rd edn, London: Macmillan.

Halsey, A H (1987), 'Social trends since World War Two', *Social Trends* 17, London: HMSO.

Harris, J. (1991) in 'Enterprise and the Welfare State', in T Gourvish and A O'Day (eds), *Britain since 1945*, London: Macmillan.

Hewitt, P (1993), *About Time: the Revolution in Work and Family Life*, London: Institute of Public Policy Research/Rivers Oram Press.

Hills, J et al. (eds) (1990), *The State of Welfare*, Oxford: Oxford University Press.

Marquand, D (1988), *The Unprincipled Society*, Fontana Press.

Murray, C (1990), *The Emerging British Underclass*, London: Institute of Economic Affairs Health and Welfare Unit.

Northcott, J (1991), *Britain in 2010: the PSI Report*, London: Policy Studies Institute.

OPCS (1992), 'Provisional mid-1991 population, estimates for England and Wales', OPCS *Monitor*, October.

Ritzer, G (1993), *The McDonaldization of Society*, Thousand Oaks, California: Pine Forge Press.

Saunders, P (1990), *A Nation of Home Owners*, London: Unwin Hyman.

Taylor Gooby, P (1991), *Social Change, Social Welfare and Social Science*, London: Harvester Wheatsheaf.

Wiener, M (1981), *English Culture and the Decline of the Industrial Spirit*, Cambridge: Cambridge University Press.

2

COMMUNICATING

It is claimed that we now live in an 'information society' where information has replaced capital and labour as one of the fundamental variables of society. Communication is a basic human activity: our ability to use language sets us apart from other animals. Recent developments, in particular the linkage between telecommunications and information technology, have revolutionized this age-old process and are comparable to other major advances in the history of communication. The invention of hieroglyphics around 3000 BC was a gigantic leap forward in human communication. The Gutenberg printing press of the fifteenth century was another as it dispensed with the need for armies of clerks laboriously transcribing documents. It established the conditions for mass literacy, although it was to take another four hundred years for this to be achieved in Western Europe. The twentieth century saw the proliferation of books, magazines and newspapers for a mass readership of millions around the globe. Although printing machines had become more sophisticated and faster they were based on the same principles as Gutenberg and still use movable type in the way that he had done. Information Technology (IT) has changed the organization, production and dissemination of the printed word. Countless jobs in the printing industry have disappeared because the skills of compositors are no longer required. Computerization has meant that text can be typed into a terminal – direct entry – and the layout and design can be done on the same machine. The text can now be transmitted around the world within seconds. The production of the printed word is but one illustration of the process which is called the 'information revolution'. Other examples are all around us: the extensive and growing use of microcomputers in home and office; the digital electronics which produced a range of 'intelligent' home appliances – washing machines, cookers, dishwashers – to name but a few. This 'information revolution' has already caused some large scale effects: there has been a reduction of jobs in many industries, indeed many jobs have simply disappeared as with the example of printing where certain tasks are now performed by computer technology. Probably the best known examples of this displacement of humans by computers are the robots which have replaced car workers on the assembly lines of car plants world-wide.

In this chapter we will examine a number of dimensions of the 'information revolution' in order to establish how the benefits of the new technology are distributed. Information Technology and telecommunications have had, are having and will continue to have considerable effects on the way we all live our everyday lives. As Vitalari sees it, IT is an inherent part of everyday life: 'all the minutiae, passions, events, goals, experiences and aspirations of human beings as they live and work, rest and play, compete and cooperate, suffer and succeed' (1991, p. 97). The Spanish sociologist, Manuel Castells, expresses it more succinctly: 'new information technologies are transforming the way we produce, consume, manage, live and die' (1989, p. 15). The changes in social life – in everyday life in households, in families and the lives of individuals – have been considerable so far although we seem to be still at the beginning of this process (see Miles et al., 1988).

Evidence suggests that while the golden promise of an IT revolution will remain unfulfilled it is incontrovertible that the advanced industrial societies are moving rapidly to a position where information is now a central component of economic life; this means that because information is now a product with a value, some people are unable to afford to buy it. It can be argued that government has a role to play in the regulation of information technology and communications to ensure that these people are not unduly disadvantaged. Similarly, the new technology can be used to overcome some of the problems which disabled and isolated people face, and government needs to support this.

Computerization has given the British state the capacity to amass enormous quantities of information on citizens. There are real fears that the considerable amount of information collected by the state on all of our lives will be used to intrude into the privacy of ordinary citizens. There is the danger that this information could be deployed against individuals by the state and it is important that there be adequate safeguards against abuse. More than this, the right to information can be seen as the precondition for the effective exercise of other rights in our society.

The Optimists: an Information Revolution

There have been three phases in the adoption of computer technology by western industrial societies since the end of the Second World War. In the first phase computers were vast machines operating in large halls and owned by giant corporations or government departments. It was reckoned in the United States in the 1950s that only eight or nine computers were needed to provide for the needs of that country:

> IBM's Mark 1, completed in January 1943 at its accounting machine plant in Endicott, New York, at a cost of half-million dollars, served Harvard University until 1959. Driven by an electric-powered drive-shaft that ran throughout machinery fifty-one feet long but only two feet wide, the 'Automatic Sequence Controlled Calculator' contained 760,000 electrical components and five hundred miles of wire. (Beniger, 1986, p. 405)

Then came the miniaturization of electronics in the 1960s and 1970s when thousands of smaller computers began to be used by companies and offices. Computer technology began to affect the work process, eliminating some repetitive tasks and improving efficiency in the processing of information, as with records systems and filing. But it was the invention of the microchip which has had the most extensive repercussions, leading to the widespread introduction of personal computers – at work and in the home. This mass availability of the micro – the microrevolution – is one of the developments which prompted much of the theorizing about a new society, largely because the scale and extent of technological innovation in computer manufacture and design has been staggering. Chris Evans in his book *The Micro Revolution* pointed out that had the automobile industry made as much progress over thirty years as had the computer industry (to the end of the 1970s), it would have been possible to buy a Rolls Royce for £1.35, get three million miles to the gallon, and be able to park six of them on a pinhead! (Evans, 1980, p. 76)

The microcomputers which are in millions of homes can perform functions that a generation ago would have only been possible for a large, mainframe machine. Household machines, and now lap top computers, have memories which twenty years ago only a mainframe possessed. But these computers are only one part of the change in technology which has got so many people talking about an 'information revolution' or 'the information society'. Information technology has been added to so many aspects of life – wrist-watches, washing machines and telephones – while calculators, video-recorders and computer games machines are only possible because of IT.

It is a simplification of the information technology and society debate to say that it has been conducted by optimists and pessimists; the issues are much more complicated and diverse than this simple dichotomy allows. Nonetheless it is a useful way of differentiating the basic positions (for a more nuanced typology see Miles, 1988). The chart below shows the quite different analyses of opposing theorists as to the effects of IT on various aspects of our society.

Optimists	Pessimists
More and better, less dangerous jobs.	Fewer jobs. Jobs will be deskilled. High unemployment.
More homeworking with subsequent advantages: less pollution and traffic congestion.	More homeworking means more privatization, loss of social contact.
More teleshopping with less pollution and traffic congestion.	More teleshopping means more privatization and individual isolation.
Greater educational opportunities through the spread of IT.	Computer literacy will restrict entry to forms of education.
Decentralization.	Greater control and centralization.
Inequalities diminish with impact of IT.	Inequalities persist, sources of wealth and power remain the same.
Greater information.	More trivia. Increasing inequality as more information has to be purchased.

Tom Stonier, Alvin Toffler and Daniel Bell are three of the leading 'optimists' and a discussion of their work enables us to evaluate the claims that are being made for the new technology. Stonier sees information technology as the latest phase in a long engagement by humankind with technology. For him the excitement rests in the fact that the computer is an extension of the brain and therefore qualitatively different from mechanical devices which extended the capacity of our muscles. Stonier believes that we are now living in a 'communicative era' which has these characteristics:

1 There is a well-developed communications infrastructure together with a sophisticated, world wide transportation system.
2 This society is now driven by its 'information economy' in which the 'knowledge industry' dominates other sectors of the economy.
3 This leads to the lessening of war as a means of resolving international conflict and the democratisation of society.
4 All cultural institutions are affected by these changes: religion, family, work, leisure etc. (Stonier, 1983, chapter 2)

Alvin Toffler also believes that we are entering an 'information society' or what he calls the 'third wave'. The rise of agriculture was the first phase or 'wave' in human development while the second wave was the change from agricultural to industrial society (Toffler, 1981). In the second wave it was human beings who communicated in industrial societies through the mass media, the post office and the telephone. But in the third wave, machines can talk to other machines or machines can talk to people. An example is the school computer which when informed of a child's absence will telephone the home and if unable to get through will persist until it can reach the parent and then deliver a message urging that parent to get the importance of school attendance across to the child (Dunlop and Kling, 1991). For Toffler the shape of the economy will change with the eventual dominance of the 'knowledge industry' which he defines as all the workers whose tasks involve them in the processing of information. It is not just computer programmers and systems analysts but also social workers, teachers and health staff. In the 'information society' knowledge has replaced capital as the major resource. Knowledge is the raw material which is used to power economic developments. Machine tools which have built-in programs to guide the pattern of work are an example. In the 'information society' large numbers of unskilled workers are not required as basic manual tasks can usually be performed by intelligent machines. Thus unemployment is a result of the transition from industrial to information society. Information workers are, however, much in demand in these societies and are a

Table 2.1 The post-industrial society: a comparative schema

Mode of production	Preindustrial extractive	Industrial–Fabrication	Postindustrial–Processing	Recycling
Economic sector	*Primary* Agriculture Mining Fishing Timber Oil and gas	*Secondary* Goods-producing Manufacturing Durables Nondurables Heavy construction	Services *Tertiary* Transportation Utilities *Quinary* Health, Education Research, Government, Recreation	*Quaternary* Trade Finance Insurance Real estate
Transforming resource	*Natural power* Wind, water, draft animal, human muscle	*Created energy* Electricity – oil, gas, coal, nuclear power	*Information* Computer and data-transmission systems	
Strategic resource	Raw materials	Financial capital	Knowledge	
Technology	Craft	Machine technology	Intellectual technology	
Skill base	Artisan, manual worker, farmer	Engineer, semiskilled worker	Scientist, technical and professional occupations	
Methodology	Common sense, trial and error, experience	Empiricism, experimentation	Abstract theory, models, simulations, decision theory, systems analysis	
Time perspective	Orientation to the past	Ad hoc adaptiveness, experimentation	Future orientation: forecasting and planning	
Design	Game against nature	Game against fabricated future	Game between persons	
Axial principle	Traditionalism	Economic growth	Codification of theoretical knowledge	

Source: Daniel Bell, 'The Information Society', in Tom Forester (ed.) (1980), The Microelectronics Revolution, Oxford: Blackwell, pp. 504–5.

fast-growing sector. In an information society the computer is the basic technology, just as the steam engine was for the industrial revolution.

In Toffler's view there is at the present time a battle going on between those who are still operating in the 'second wave', that is to say, industrial society and those who are proponents of the 'third wave'. This is really the point of the Toffler thesis, namely, that we are entering a new age of information technology or an 'information society'. Capitalism and socialism are both industrial ideologies and will not be appropriate for the emerging society. The site of production is not the office or the factory but the home. Production for use will return as the dominant economic form – what he calls 'prosuming'. This will lead to a weakening of the market: Toffler believes that the 'marketization' of the world has been completed anyway and firmly attributes this to the second (industrial) wave. There will be an increasing decentralization of economic activity made possible by the widespread introduction of information technology. This will enable the flourishing of teleworking and the focus of economic activity will become the home or the 'electronic cottage'.

Daniel Bell provides the most sophisticated account of the information society (1973, 1980). His account centres on three features: a change from goods-producing societies to service societies; the central importance of theoretical knowledge for the development of technology; and the creation of a new intellectual technology (Bell, 1980b, p. 501). Bell points out that jobs in manufacturing industries in western economies are in manifest decline while those in what he terms 'human services', by which he means social services, teaching and 'professional services', are on the increase. Knowledge has replaced capital as a crucial variable in production because it can be applied in order to transform resources as with a particular invention or technological innovation. Bell distinguishes between information and knowledge: information is data while knowledge is 'an organized set of statements of fact or ideas, presenting a reasoned judgement or an experimental result, which is transmitted to others through some communication medium in some systematic form' (Bell, 1980b, pp. 505–6). His account is summarized in table 2.1.

Proponents of the information society thesis equate it with human progress. It will lead, seemingly inexorably, to less centralized control as people are able to pass information around the system on a horizontal basis. Decentralization is a natural concomitant in industrial and service organizations. Indeed this is happening with a real change in the form of multinational corporations to more decentralized forms of operation, but it is doubtful whether the locus of control has changed.

The optimists' belief is that IT will open up many opportunities for direct democracy as citizens are able to vote 'on-line' via their home-computers, or cable TV, on issues of local and national importance. Equally, education will dramatically change as students will be enabled via hypertext systems to access vast quantities of infor-mation. Teachers will see their role redefined as guides to this information being purveyed by multimedia systems. The arrival of expert systems, computers which have been programmed with the specialized knowledge of doctors or lawyers or other experts and thus can be used to provide diagnoses or opinions for more junior staff, means that problems can be taken to a computer for solution. The computer asks a series of questions in order to reach its verdict. Expert systems have been most widely developed in medicine and law. The most exciting breakthrough will be the arrival of computers which can think for themselves and make better decisions than most humans.

Pessimists

But is information society so different from an industrial society? The raw materials may not be the same but does not control rest in the hands of the same corporations and governments who dominated industrial society? This is the view of the pessimists. The distinction made here between optimists and pessimists hides the fact that both groups differ internally on their views on the impact of information technology. This is certainly the case with the pessimists who, nonetheless, can be grouped together because they all, at least, share a scepticism regarding the claims of the proponents of information society. Generally the pessimist position is distinguished by its view that the information technology optimists completely ignore the socio-economic context in which the technology is being introduced. The optimists are regarded as technological determinists, i.e. they see the technology itself as leading to widespread change just as the steam engine did or the wheel, while the pessimists want to argue that economic and political structures determine in large part how it will be used.

The nub of the pessimist case is that information technology is like any other product and will therefore be used by the powerful interests in society in order to improve their own interests, power and control. In the case of information technology the multinational corporations are seen as major players who can displace labour by using much more sophisticated machinery thereby cutting costs. Multinationals also predominate in the world of information technology equipment, hardware and software and have great influence with governments, all of whom want to persuade them that they should locate in their countries. The pessimists remark on how close the links are between the defence and the information technology industries. These links were most clearly revealed in the 1980s when American President Ronald Reagan announced the 'Star Wars' project, officially known as the Strategic Defence Initiative, involving many prominent defence contractors and designed to provide a huge protective shield against incoming nuclear missiles, using super-computers and lasers (Thompson and Smith, 1985). This project, since abandoned as technologically impossible, was only the most ambitious and expensive of a continuing stream of US government contracts for high tech defence and armaments products which has stimulated the growth of IT (and several multinationals) in the USA.

Multinational companies are the prime movers in the information economy (Schiller, 1984). They have pushed since the 1970s for an end to the national postal and telecommunication authorities to be found in western Europe and for them to be replaced by privatized telecommunication companies. The other thrust of their activity has been to commercialize information. Information is now an important commodity which can be bought and sold in the market. The big multinationals aim to control the pathways by which this information is transmitted around the world and Schiller points out that sometimes the ambitions of these companies conflict with the sovereignty of nation states. The companies believe in the international flow of information, in effect a free market in information with the content of the information left to the provider. They maintain that they and not government agencies should run these global networks (p. 9).

The American media and computer corporations – often the same business – have been insistent on the need for free information flows or 'free trade' in information but understandably many governments do not see it this way. In the 1970s and 1980s Third World governments, in particular, were keen that there be some control on the dissemination of information and communications. They feared that one world-view, that of the industrialized West, was being promulgated around the globe and crowding out alternative ways of thinking. This resulted in the publication of the UNESCO report, *Many Voices, One World*, known as the MacBride Report, after its President Sean MacBride. He remarked that 'free flow' was often only one way, from the North to the South: 'this flow (data, messages, media programmes, cultural products) is directed predominantly from bigger to smaller countries, from those with power and technological means towards those less advanced, from the developed to the developing world and, on the national level, from the power centre downwards' (1980, p. 145). The MacBride Report recommended that preference should be given to non-commercial forms of media when their expansion was being considered and that developing countries should establish national cultural policies to protect them from being swamped by Western providers, and called on Western countries to foster the spread of technical information to the poor world (pp. 260–2).

Nevertheless, despite the publication of the report in 1980, the multinationals' globalization of communication has increased apace. In Western Europe several large media conglomerates have emerged which predominate in the world of television, press and printed communications. These are transnational in operation and have utilized the introduction of satellite broadcasting and cable television to enhance and extend their spheres of operation. Pessimists point to the range of programmes provided by satellite television as confirmation of their fears about the content of the information being purveyed. These are mass programmes for a mass audience treated as consumers of information.

The privatization of information is a real concern to the pessimists. Schiller contrasts the model of the public library, essentially invented in the last century, with the access to information in the late twentieth century which is increasingly done on a 'pay per' system in which the viewer pays a fee for each television channel or service (Schiller and Schiller, 1988) (see p. 66 below). Libraries are subject to strong pressures to restrict their principle of free access and they are coming under great commercial competition. There has been a gigantic increase in information recently, especially in the areas of science and technology, and public libraries find it difficult to keep pace with this. The commercialization of information has occurred in the UK. From the early years of the Thatcher government a decision was made to charge much higher prices for government publications. In 1983 the government's report on Information Technology was simply entitled *Making a Business of Information* (Cabinet Office, 1983). In the public library system the introduction of charges has occurred although the basic service is still free. But a library service short of money finds it increasingly difficult to keep abreast of the new forms of information provision, for instance it is very expensive to provide on-line searching. Unfortunately the way in which the public library system is developing as a second-class purveyor of information seems to symbolize the position of public provision.

Spatial Inequalities

Until the twentieth century distance had always been a problem in communication, but this is no longer true. Information technology reduces distances since it enables almost immediate communication to take place across the globe. IT has also changed the relationship between individuals and time. Distances have become progressively shorter in the twentieth century because of major technological developments such as the jet engine, while information technology enables almost simultaneous transmission of data around the world via the facsimile machine (fax). These technological developments produce the phenomenon which has been referred to as 'time–space compression': in a real sense, of course, distances cannot get shorter but the time needed to travel between two points and to transmit information has been dramatically reduced. The dominant business and financial groups have created private electronic highways around the globe. At the same time for some people, for example those without access to personal transport, distances have been getting longer.

Business and financial interests have dominated the provision of information technology since the early 1980s. Government policy since 1979 has been to enable private sector developments to go ahead but not, unlike some other Western European governments, to lead the telecommunications and information technologies industries by giving substantial investment finance to projects regarded as in the national interest. World-wide, traditional centres of finance capital have become the major growth points for the expansion of infor-mation technology. The technology has been extremely useful in the internationalization of the money markets linking New York, Tokyo and London on a continuous basis so that it is possible to trade on the stock exchanges of the world twenty-four hours a day. As a result it is the big cities which are being 'wired up' for the new technology and there are real fears that backward regions will be omitted from this development. Developments in Britain have mainly been led by the private sector. In the 1980s the privatization of British Telecom was a decisive event for it accentuated its orientation towards business customers. In the 1980s calls for private subscribers became dearer and the calls for long-distance users, mainly business, became cheaper. The monopoly was broken by the arrival of Mercury as an alternative telecommunications company but this too is orientated towards the needs of the private sector, not the private subscriber. However, this duopoly is to be ended with the announcement by the government in 1991 that by the middle of the decade customers should be able to have a much greater choice as to who will supply their telephone service. The government decided that the cable TV companies should be able to offer telephone services themselves (Department of Trade and Industry, 1991). ISDN is being supplied in this country to link major business centres with large parts of the country excluded. The same is true of the location of teleports: there are two in London Docklands linked to world-wide satellite communication. These private monopolies and government have not shown great interest in extending the new information technology/telecommunication routes to other parts of the country.

The optimists believe that information technology will become a universal resource to be used by all, like water or energy. But there is little sign so far of this. Regions and cities which have high concentrations of information workers are able to participate in the new information services and markets while there seems to be an 'information gap' opening up between 'information rich' and 'information poor' regions. Hepworth and Robins have illustrated this process at work in the North East of England. They are sceptical whether regions such as the North East, which played a key part in the industrial development of England, will be able to play any significant role in an information economy because information technology developments are attracted to the prosperous regions. This becomes a crucial issue if the regeneration of industrial Britain is to depend upon access to information technology. There is a view that there will be a 'trickle-down' effect with the 'informatization' of the economy but this might take some considerable time, during which the poor regions will have become even more stagnant and it may prove impossible to produce an economic revival. It can be seen that it really is important that information technology developments are not absent from a region when one bears in mind that the information economy has been characterized as one where there is 'a *new* phase of economic development, whereby the production of

Table 2.2 Information occupations in the British workforce by region (1981–86)

	Share of information occupations in labour force (1981)[a] (percent)	Unemployment rate (1986)[b] (percent)	Share of information occupations in total employment (1986)[c] (percent)
Great Britain	45.2	11.5	40.0
South East	47.4	8.7	43.3
East Anglia	41.6	8.9	37.9
Greater London	58.0	9.7	52.4
South West	43.8	10.0	39.4
West Midlands	42.1	14.0	36.2
East Midlands	41.0	11.3	36.4
Yorkshire and Humberside	40.4	13.7	34.9
North West	43.9	14.5	37.5
North	38.9	16.8	32.4
Wales	39.5	14.1	34.0
Scotland	40.2	14.3	34.5

Source: M Hepworth and K Robins (1988), 'Whose information society?', *Media Culture and Society*, 10, p. 331.
[a] Hepworth, M, Green, A, and Gillespie, A (1987), 'The Spatial Division of Information Labour in Great Britain', *Environment and Planning*, 19, pp. 793–806.
[b] *Department of Employment Gazette*, August 1986.
[c] The incidence of unemployment is assumed to be undifferentiated across occupations.

goods and services dominates wealth and job creation with computers and telecommunications providing the technological potential for product and process innovation' (Hepworth, 1989, p. 7). As table 2.2 shows there is a regional imbalance in the employment of information workers between regions. Hepworth and Robins characterize this as an 'information occupation gap' (1988, p. 334).

There were substantial job losses in the North of England during the 1980s as the old manufacturing industries shut down, whereas two thirds of the new service jobs which were created were in South East England (Hepworth and Robins, 1988, p. 334). This reveals that the socio-political process operates in such a way that it is very difficult, many would say impossible, for declining regions to break into the new world of telecommunications and information technology without a government-backed regional policy. The introduction of the optical cable network in the United Kingdom is an example of this. Fibre optics enable much greater volumes of telecommunications traffic to be relayed and more extensive range of services to be offered to users. British Telecom has been very slow in introducing this new technology because of the large costs involved. Yet in the late 1980s the European Commission provided a grant of £7.25 million for the introduction of an optical cable network in Northern Ireland which persuaded British Telecom that it should spend the extra £100 million needed (Large, 1990).

Policies for 'technology transfer' are about supplying new information technologies to small and medium size firms who will make use of them. It is clear that these issues are pertinent to Social policy for they involve the distribution of opportunities to backward regions and to disadvantaged groups. They are issues relating to access to the basic infrastructure of a modern society. In a world where information technology has been appropriated by transnational corporations then it is increasingly difficult for peripheral regions to hold their own in the 'information economy'. What they want to avoid is becoming assembly plants for goods manufactured elsewhere in the world. There is a very strong counter-argument to Toffler that mass communication and, by extension, information technology is inherently centralizing. It enables one capital to dominate a less favoured region.

In his most popular book, *The Third Wave* (1981), Toffler uses the term 'electronic cottage' to describe the location of much of the work that will be done in the information society. In truth, it really does not look as though this is likely to occur as for some time the rural areas have been left out of the spread of information technology networks: IT developments have been in the urban conurbations with associated developments in the surrounding regions. It is the peripheral parts of the United Kingdom and indeed Western Europe which have lost out in this process. An example of how information technology can be used to overcome the traditional isolation of rural communities has been demonstrated by a project in Scandinavian countries: Community Teleservice Centres. Their role is to equip villages with access to data processing and telecommunications as well as other computer assisted services, and they have been established in more than 50 locations in Denmark, Norway, Finland and Sweden (Glastonbury, 1990). In practice this means that for the community's use there are personal computers, printers, modems and video equipment for production as well as software of a wide description. Teleservice Centres are not without problems for many people in rural areas do not have the training or knowledge to use them. The idea has now been taken up in the UK, although here the accent has been more on the possibility of starting 'telebusinesses' in rural areas. The Highlands and Islands Development Board has invested in the provision of computer and ISDN links from this remote region to the rest of the UK (Tilley, 1990).

The Potential of IT to Improve the Quality of Life

Many people in our society find it difficult to communicate because they have a disability: they might be blind, partially sighted or have a hearing problem. In some ways modern communications have exacerbated the difficulties they experience. Profoundly deaf people cannot use the ordinary telephone so they find it difficult to keep in touch with people or do the ordinary everyday tasks that are essential but most of us do not consider to be problematic – like ringing up the Gas Board. Employment becomes harder to obtain if you cannot use the phone, and once in work then it is a serious limitation for a person. In the UK it is estimated that at least 200,000 people are unable to use the phone even if it is amplified (Jones, 1990). It is one of the ironies of the introduction of information technology that while it was claimed that the computer screens and telecommunications links would introduce the 'paperless office', in practice what seems to have happened is that more paper has been generated by the technology than was produced before. Clearly, blind and partially sighted people have real difficulties coping with this form of information, as do the estimated 10 per cent of the population who, although they have all their senses, have difficulties with reading and writing.

Elderly people have specific communication problems if they suffer from a sensory handicap, or they may have a physical handicap which confines them to the home and as a result become much more dependent on modern means of communication. There are now a variety of add-on devices for the telephone which are designed to help people with particular handicaps: for example, the telephone can be amplified for outgoing speech for people with very weak voices. For people with no speech at all then there is a device called Claudius Converse which consists of a key-pad connected to the phone which can 'speak' up to 64 phrases, in either a male or female voice, at the touch of the button. Profoundly deaf people can use the phone with a text terminal. This is a keyboard and screen on which you can type your message which can then be sent to someone who has the same equipment. Of course the number of people who have this equipment is very limited and as a result British Telecom operate a relay service whereby calls can be made via an operator who will read out the messages and then type into their terminal the other person's reply (British Telecom, 1991).

Cost is a restraining, and very frustrating feature of all the technological developments for disabled people which have emerged in the past decade. A recent survey considered the extent to which there was a demand among elderly and disabled people for technological aids to help communication. The author concluded that elderly people and disabled people were not very interested in this technology. It was the cost which deterred them:

> It is impossible to avoid the conclusion that many of the offerings in the British Telecom brochure were seen as little more than fantasy. For example, although there was interest in the large number dial, the £15 charge to fit a 'free' dial would immediately have deterred the respondents. Even the simplest devices on offer were beyond consideration for the vast majority of the elderly, and for most of the disabled, because of their cost, including installation cost. (Tinker, 1990)

For some severely disabled people microtechnology offers the chance to work and to participate in a wide range of activities. The computer can now, using a speech synthesizer, speak on the instructions of the disabled person. Stephen Hawking, the Lucasian Professor of Mathematics at the University of Cambridge, is probably the best known user of one of these systems. He has motor-neurone disease and is unable to speak naturally but is able using a speech synthesizer to write and lecture to great effect. His best-selling book on the origins of the universe *A Brief History of Time* was written using this technology. Many other disabled people with speech difficulties use a variety of technological devices which become more sophisticated each year. There are now devices, available to help people with profound speech problems, which are 'predictive': they are able to predict the words which are most likely to come next in a sequence and then offer them as a one key alternative to the user spelling out the word. Unfortunately health and social services are not organized to give help and assistance to adults who need technical advice and support for these systems. Much of this comes from voluntary organizations, charities and user groups.

In Social Services Departments the most common use for information technology until the early 1990s was for client information and filing systems. In 1990 with the passing of the NHS and Community Care Act which introduced care management there emerged a clear need for regular information management systems so that the resources available to care managers and the costs of those resources could be assessed easily. This is essential if the new system of care management is to work for it requires up-to-the-minute information on resources as well as their cost, and this can only be supplied by an IT system.

In social work the major use of computer technology has been for management purposes. The uses of information technology for the empowerment of clients has lagged behind and is not well developed (see Glastonbury, 1985; Glastonbury and La Mendola, 1992). Nonetheless various schemes have been introduced which are extremely useful for individual people. Among these we can list the growing use of electronic alarms which can be activated when a solitary older person falls in their home; the use of telecommunications equipment to help speech-impaired people to communicate; and the way in which IT can be used by bedbound or chairbound people to control a range of devices such as central heating controls as well as television and the stereo.

Information technology has obvious benefits for social security claimants, as welfare benefits packages are in existence which enable them to establish which benefits they are entitled to and to guide them through the complexities of a complicated system. However, a recent study of the computerization programme introduced by the Department of Social Security in the 1980s concluded that the major result had been gains for the organization in terms of speed and accuracy of work. While this is undoubtedly important for claimants the authors point out that a 'bottom up' approach to computerization would also have empowered them:

> By enabling claimants to check their own entitlement through advice packages, by providing them routinely with breakdowns of benefit calculations, and with clear explanations of why decisions have been reached, they would have increased knowledge of their own social security status and of the relationship between their circumstances and their entitlement, and would thus have an increased ability to identify errors and to challenge decisions. (Adler and Sainsbury, 1991, pp. 242–3)

Privacy

Pessimists see the general introduction of information technology as part of an extension of control over the lives of the populations of the advanced world. The technology allows multinational corporations to target consumers much more precisely than in the past. The largest data base on individual consumers is the 'Nationwide Consumer File' which has information on forty-three million individuals together with their home addresses organized according to postcodes. It is an amalgamation of innumerable mailing lists combined with the electoral register to produce a complex data base which aims to supply lists of households according to their lifestyle and spending patterns (Campbell and Connor, 1986, pp. 36–7). Clearly the main use of this information is for companies wishing to target their products by use of mail-shots. Nonetheless it is claimed that it is used by private detective agencies and this can be seen as an erosion of privacy.

In recent years the police have used computer networks to increase greatly their ability to monitor the public. It was revealed by a Commons Select Committee in 1990 that half a million people had been vetted the previous year using the Police National Computer. Clearly most people would be in agreement with the practice, which means that checks are run on people who will have access to classified material of national importance and other categories such as people who are going to work with children as employees of Social Services departments, police force applicants, potential jurors in cases involving national security and the like (Pienaar, 1990). The Police National Computer deals with a staggering volume of enquiries each year: in 1986 it was claimed that it was used to check eleven million or so people and nineteen million vehicles (Campbell and Connor, 1986, pp. 227–8). There have been instances where inaccurate or untrue information has been placed on the PNC which has labelled a person as a subversive and thus barred them from certain forms of employment.

Surveillance of the population is something which we associate with 'Big Brother' or science fiction fantasies yet the advent of information technology has meant that the systems are now available, if not in place, to monitor the population on a scale never before possible. The telephone system in this country now automatically records the time and duration of each call together with the number dialled. This information can be used to track down and identify the calls of particular individuals – clearly something which is of great value to the security services. Our movements each day, our telephone calls, our meetings with others, our places of entertainment and our shopping are not all of interest to any one person or body but together they are trails which show what we are doing with our lives. This is what has been called 'transactional information' (Burnham, 1983). Various items of this information are of interest to different organizations. Clearly retailers will be most interested in the credit card transactions of various socioeconomic groups. The advent of computerized home shopping will mean that retailers will be able to monitor the shopping choices of homeshoppers in an extremely precise way – every product ordered can be linked directly to the customer so that through time a 'profile' of this shopper is built up. The introduction of Electronic Point of Sale (EPOS) – the light pens that read the bar codes – in so many shops means that a very large amount of information on consumer purchases is built up.

Banks are another massive information resource which have used computers to enhance their efficiency greatly but at the same time the information collected can be of great use to the police or security services if they are tracking an individual. The most obvious example of tracking is the introduction on a trial basis in this country of electronic tagging for clients of Probation Officers to make sure that they do not abscond. This has now been legalized in the Criminal Justice Act 1991. The Data Protection Act 1984 gives British citizens the right to obtain all information held on them by a computer. But this Act does not put the onus on the information gatherer to inform the person that such information is held! There are a variety of ways in which the right of individuals under this Act to see data collected about them by organizations or firms can be evaded. The most straightforward is to transfer the material to paper, from the computer to the filing cabinet. It is a time consuming and expensive business obtaining this information and the Registrar for Data Protection does not have extensive powers to ensure that the Act is properly complied with (Campbell and Connor, 1986, chapter 7).

The welfare state is a huge information store: social security records, national health service information, housing records, education records; put together these amount to a great deal of information on each individual. Computerization makes it much easier for government departments to assemble, store and hold information about citizens. In many ways this is more efficient and works for the benefit of the user. Sub-offices of the Housing Department all have access, via the computer screen, to central information about tenants and so can help enquirers much more easily when they come into the office. District nurses now record information in patients' homes on handheld sets which can then be used later. It is estimated that in Britain each year civil servants open two million new files and deal with 86,000 official forms (Roberts and Rowlands, 1991, p. 49). Much of this is routine clerical data which is of no possible interest to anyone. Some, say on social security records, may be of a highly sensitive nature, perhaps concerning personal relationships, which could be very damaging for an individual if it were to enter the public domain. One of the major dangers is the linking of various national computers so that they exchange information between one another. The new Department of Social Security computer has been designed around a 'central index' holding information on almost every citizen compiled from the records of the Department of Social Security and the Inland Revenue. There are fears that this enormous information store could provide a register of the entire population of the UK which would be linked to an identity card system, based on the National Insurance numbercards (Campbell and Connor, 1986, chapter 4). There is a real problem when this information is inaccurate or, quite simply, untrue and yet the person concerned does not even know that the record has been checked. There have been a number of worrying cases where security checks run on people applying for jobs in public institutions such as the BBC have revealed that they are considered to be 'subversives' although the extent of their political activities may have been confined to membership of a left wing student society twenty years before! (Hollingsworth and Taylor, 1988)

Technology has considerably eased information gathering, the facility with which information can be stored and the speed by which it can be transmitted. It has made for much greater efficiency. There remains, however, a fear that the immense information storage capacity of the state and private business will be used in harmful ways. This has existed since the dawn of the computer age in the 1940s and was given powerful expression by George Orwell in his book *1984* where the state induced social conformity by its ability to watch citizens at all times. In Britain this fear has been given some nourishment in the 1980s as a number of press reports have disclosed the huge data gathering capacities of the police and their ability with the help of modern technology to record thousands of telephone conversations (see Manwaring-White, 1983). It is most commonly the security services, MI5 and the Special Branch, who are accused of collecting this kind of unnecessary information. *Spycatcher*, the book by former MI5 officer Peter Wright, which the British government tried so hard to stop being published, gives an account of how a section of MI5 tried to destabilize Labour governments. Although the account has been challenged, what is not in dispute is the amount of sophisticated electronic bugging equipment which lay at the disposal of Wright and other officers. As he writes: 'For five years we bugged and burgled our way across London at the state's behest while pompous bowler-hatted civil servants in Whitehall pretended to look the other way' (Wright, 1987).

The practice of democratic politics so essential to the health of a complex, industrial society can be weakened by the illicit use of such information. Allegations were subsequently made that at the time of the 1983 General Election government ministers had access, via the security services, to the telephone conversations of their opponents, principally the leadership of CND, in the great debate that was in progress then on national defence centring on the possession of nuclear weapons by the UK government (Campbell and Connor, 1986, pp. 283–4). Such incidents induce a scepticism about the potential of computerization for the advancement of democracy.

Information as a Right

Steele argues that information is important as it enables citizens to:

1 participate in decision making and democracy and to ensure that institutions are accountable
2 fulfil their duties, rights and responsibilities and make sure they get the services which they are entitled to
3 look after themselves and to make informed choices about their lives. (Steele, 1991, p. 47)

The National Consumer Council (NCC) has argued that there is a *right* to information and advice – it is a right to be set alongside the legal, civil and social rights we enjoy. Golding and Murdock agree, arguing that citizenship is not a reality unless there is an addition to this concept of social rights, namely, the rights of universal access to communications and information facilities' (1991, p. 36). For they insist that people should have access to information that enables them to make sense of their rights, to know what they are. In addition, they believe that citizens should have access to the broadest possible range of information and interpretation of this information. But their conception is more extensive than the NCC for they want access to communication facilities, which presumably means access to computer and telecommunications equipment. As we shall see in the chapter on broadcasting the shift from public to private control of the mass media works against this principle.

Given the way in which there has been a move away from single providers in the local and central state services then it is apparent that individuals need good information more than ever before in order that they can make an informed choice. Examples abound: how does one decide which is the best old people's home for a relation? Who can provide cleaning services for an isolated elderly person? Over the years health authorities and social services departments, as well as other sectors of local government which interact directly with people each day, have made efforts to increase their information to the public. Recent studies show that 'people do not have much idea about where to go for help on these topics and make little use of formal information sources' (Moore and Steele, 1991, p. 129). It would appear that when people have problems which concern the social services, rather than turn directly to the statutory agency they will seek first the advice of friends, families and neighbours, although as Moore and Steele point out these people are often unable to give adequate advice because of the complexity of the issues. In a society like ours it is not possible to get through the maze of life without information and assistance on how to use that information. The Consumers' Association provide an impartial scrutiny of consumer goods with their publication, *Which?* Many have argued that there is a need for a similar impartial advice and information agency for the scrutiny of state services.

Access to Information

The move from public provision, via the public library service or the government department, to private provision through the company which specializes in the sale of information has consequences for the lives of all of us. Research companies routinely gather data about the habits, opinions and, most commonly, spending patterns of the population but they will only release this information at a high price and it is normally only companies which can afford to purchase it. In contrast, the public library service is organized in order to give everyone access to information, although some kind of residence qualification is usually imposed for the borrowing of books. But the public library dates from the pre-information age of the nineteenth century when information was not a commodity. Although libraries in this country have made valiant efforts to keep up to date with the new technologies of information – CD roms and on-line systems – the cost of information is a deterrent to all but the best funded, just as it is to most citizens.

'Hello, Emily. This is Gladys Murphy up the street. Fine, thanks . . . say, could you go to your window and describe what's in my front yard?'

Source: The Economist, 4 May 1991. Copyright © Universal Press Syndicate; reproduced by permission.

The Role of Government

Privatization was one of the key themes of the 1980s under the Conservative government of Margaret Thatcher. The largest public utility to be privatized was British Telecom in 1984. It was supposed to usher in a new era of 'people's capitalism' in which the man in the street would be a shareholder as well as a motorist and an owner occupier. Although a large number of small shareholders did emerge, very many of them making a substantial profit when they sold their shares, the real bonus for BT was that, freed of government control, it could develop its business in a straightforward commercial direction. This resulted in an increase in charges for the domestic user, not a very profitable part of the service, and a reduction in charges for business users who were, correctly, targetted as a source of high profits in the future for BT. The losses on local calls used to be subsidized by the profits on long-distance calls but this practice was ended in 1982. The privatization of information can be seen in the services offered in the phone book. In the past directory enquiries was a free service as was the weather report. Now subscribers have to pay for both these services. This is to say nothing of the burgeoning range of other information services available to subscribers.

It is a truism that the telephone can be a lifeline for elderly and disabled people who live on their own. Indeed, the Chronically Sick and Disabled Persons Act 1970 allowed local authority Social Services Departments to pay for the cost of installing a phone for isolated elderly and disabled people. Wenger argues that the provision of a telephone to an elderly person living alone is important in the new strategy of community care, 'reducing risk, enhancing social contact and making continued care in the community more likely' (1992, p. 19). Yet still today there are four million households that do not have a telephone (Golding and Murdock, 1991). This means that they are cut off not only from contact with friends and families who live at some distance, but in addition the growing range of services which our phone links us to, from dial-a-disc to the chat lines to the various 0898 (Freefone) numbers. The media assume that possession of the phone is universal. Witness the children's programmes which have quizzes requiring viewers to phone in their answers. Those great national events of the media age, the telethons, are only possible because of the credit card, the television and the telephone. A telephone and communications organization which was informed in its policy by social priorities might believe that the provision of phones to the four million homes without one was a priority. A commercial company cannot pursue this policy – besides, the new, mainly low income subscribers would not be great users of the various services which BT now offers.

British Telecom was one example of the government's emphasis on privatization. Another was the view, reflected in the report *Making a Business of Information*, that information was a commodity and should be treated as such, bought and sold, marketed and packaged. The stance of the Conservative government in the 1980s was that the private sector should develop the new information technologies. This has meant that the United Kingdom has not seen a system of optical-fibre cabling introduced. In the UK the considerable potential of videotext services has not been realized as it has been in France where the government, having decided in the early 1980s that it would sponsor IT developments, has borne the cost of introducing videotext and other systems.

Social Inequality

It is clear that the inequalities of the information age need to be tackled before they become an inbuilt and accepted feature. Private companies, even those with a well-developed sense of social responsibility, cannot be expected to do this. In this country the Conservative government of the 1980s left much of the development of the IT infrastructure to the private sector. As a result, entertainment systems were given a high priority because they provided the highest rate of return on profit. Other more socially useful projects such as information systems and home terminals for information and shopping did not develop because of the lack of government investment. Whether it should always be central government that provides the investment for these decisions is open to question. Experience from other countries in the 1980s suggests that investment is best supplied by a lower tier of government which is more in tune with the needs of the city or region. Certainly central government needs to supply the large sums needed for the development of ISDN or other comparable extensions of the telecommunications network. Funding has also to be given to other sections of local authorities – to Social Services Departments for instance – so that ample funds are available for the purchase of computers. Local authorities have tried over the years to come up with IT sector plans but their work has been small-scale because of the opposition of central government to these initiatives. Primarily this work has also been about attracting or promoting the formation of IT companies. But this is largely an activity in which local governments all over the world have been engaged and so the chances of attracting firms to locate in a specific part of the UK are very small.

Despite the best efforts and inclinations of so many people in the computing industry the social development of computer technology has lagged far behind that for defence, entertainment and business. The term coined to describe this privatization of information is 'the pay per' society (see Mosco and Wasko, 1988). It is a reference to the fact that payment is required for many television channels, phone facilities and information. As we shall see in the next chapter this proliferation of new broadcasting services is provided by the private sector. In Britain the state has opted out of the role of main provider and in the case of satellite television there is no state involvement whatsoever so that the satellite television channels beamed into British homes are the product of international media conglomerates.

Information technology has clearly produced considerable changes in our society and is certain to create even more far reaching changes in the future. The optimists' view of the social impact of IT which sees social inequalities disappearing because of the new technology is not borne out by the evidence reviewed here. Indeed the potential for state surveillance of the population has been massively increased by computerization. The possibilities for communication are now immense: there is an array of products which help us to communicate – carphones, cordless phones, electronic mail, fax, computers with modems – but there are barriers to their use and diffusion, particularly among the disadvantaged. Access to information, and indeed a right to information, are of greatest importance to those with the least power in our society.

Discussion Questions

1 Why have the social applications of information technology been relatively underdeveloped?
2 What are the ramifications of a 'right to information'? How could this be enforced?

Further Reading

The key issues in the debate on the impact of information technology – access, surveillance, control and technological determinism – are covered in Ruth Finnegan et al. (eds), Information Technology: social issues, (Open University Press, 1987). On surveillance and its dangers a good source is Duncan Campbell and Steve Connor, On the Record (Michael Joseph, London, 1986). The impact of IT on advanced industrial societies is surveyed in Ian Miles et al., Information Horizons: the long-term social implications of new information technologies (Edward Elgar, 1988). David Lyon, The Information Society: issues and illusions (Polity Press, 1988) is an excellent critical account. Bryan Glastonbury and Walter La Mendola, The Integrity of Intelligence: a Bill of Rights for the Information Age (Macmillan, 1992) sets out an ethical framework for the development of IT.

References

Adler, M and Sainsbury, R (1991), 'The Social Shaping of Information Technology: computerisation and the administration of social security' in Michael Adler et al. (eds), *The Sociology of Social Security*, Edinburgh: Edinburgh University Press.

Bell, D (1973), *The Coming of Post Industrial Society*, New York: Basic Books.

Bell, D (1980), *Sociological Journeys: Essays 1960–1980*, London: Heinemann.

Bell, D (1980b), 'The Social Framework of the Information Society' in T. Forester (ed.), *The Microelectronics Revolution*, Oxford: Basil Blackwell.

Beniger, J R (1986), *The Control Revolution*, London: Harvard University Press.

British Telecom (1991), *British Telecom's Guide to Equipment and Services for Disabled Customers*, London.

Burnham, D (1983), *The Rise of the Computer State*, London: Weidenfeld and Nicolson.

Cabinet Office, Information Technology Advisory Panel (1983), *Making a Business of Information*, London: HMSO.

Campbell, D and Connor, S (1986), *On the Record: Surveillance, Computers and Privacy – the Inside Story*, London: Michael Joseph.

Castells, M (1989), *The Informational City*, Oxford: Basil Blackwell.

Department of Trade and Industry (1991), *Competition and Choice: Telecommunications Policy for the 1990s*, London: HMSO.

Dunlop, C and Kling, R (1991), *Computerisation and Controversy, Value Conflicts and Social Choices*, London: Academic Press.

Evans, C (1980), *The Mighty Micro*, London: Coronet Books.

Glastonbury, B (1985), *Computers and Social Work*, London:Macmillan.

Glastonbury, B (1990), 'Community Teleservice Centres', *New Technology in the Human Services*, 5, 1, Summer.

Glastonbury, B and La Mendola, W (1992), *The Integrity Intelligence: a Bill of Rights for the Information Age*, London: Macmillan.

Golding, P and Murdock, G (1986), 'Unequal information: access and exclusion in the communications market place', in Margaret Ferguson, *New Communication Technologies and the Public Interest*, London: Sage.

Golding, P and Murdock, C (1991) 'Screening out the Poor', in J Willis and T Wollen (eds), *The Neglected Audience*, London: British Film Institute.

Hepworth, M (1989), *Geography of the Information Economy*, London: Belhaven Press.

Hepworth, M and Robins, K (1988), 'Whose information society? A view from the periphery', *Media, Culture and Society*, 10, pp. 323–43.

Hollingsworth, M and Taylor, R N (1988), 'MI5: building empires, ruining careers', *Guardian*, 6 September.

Jones, L (1990), 'Waiting for a Phone Call', *Community Care*, 19 July.

Large, P (1990), *Guardian*, 5 March.

MacBride, S (1980), International Commission for the Study of Communication Problems, *Many Voices, One World*, London: Kogan Page.

Manwaring-White, S (1983), *The Policing Revolution: Police Technology, Democracy and Liberty in Britain*, Brighton: Harvester Press.

Miles, I (1988), *Information Technology and Information Society: Options for the Future*, London: Economic and Social Research Council.

Miles, I et al. (1988), *Information Horizons: the long-term social implications of new information technology*, Aldershot: Edward Elgar.

Moore, N and Steele, J (1991), *Information Intensive Britain: an analysis of the policy issues*, London: Policy Studies Institute.

Mosco, V and Wasko, J (eds) (1988), *The Political Economy of Information*, London: University of Wisconsin Press.

Pienaar, J (1990), 'Whitehall vets half a million people', *Independent*, 16 April.

Roberts, S and Rowlands, I (1991), 'Freedom of Information: a practical perspective', *Policy Studies*, Summer, 12 (2), pp. 40–51.

Schiller, H (1984), *Information and the Crisis Economy*, New Jersey: Ablex.

Schiller, H and Schiller, A (1988), 'Libraries, Public Access to Information and Commerce', in V Mosco and J Wasko (eds), *The Political Economy of Information*, London: University of Wisconsin Press.

Steele, J (1991), 'Information for citizens', *Policy Studies*, Autumn.

Stonier, Tom (1983), *The Wealth of Information*, London: Methuen.

Thompson, E P and Smith, D (eds) (1985), *Star Wars*, Harmondsworth: Penguin.

Tilley, L (1990), 'Crofters join the electronic village', *The Times*, 10 May.

Tinker, A (1990), *The Telecommunication Needs of Elderly and Disabled People*, Office of Telecommunications.

Toffler, A (1981), *The Third Wave*, London: Pan.

Vitalari, N P (1991), 'Information Technology in Daily Life', in J Berleur et al. (eds), *The Information Society: Evolving Landscapes*, Springer Verlag.

Wenger, G Clare (1992), *Access to Cars and Telephones in Old Age: keeping in touch in rural areas*, Centre for Social Policy Research and Development, University of Wales, Bangor.

Wright, Peter (1987), *Spycatcher*, London: Heinemann.

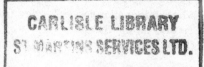

3

VIEWING

Television is the major means by which our society thinks about issues and discusses them. At its best it is a medium which enables society to talk to itself. Television's importance to social policy is clearly considerable, for it can have a direct influence through the presentation of social problems – whether this be in dramatic or documentary form – while the day to day discussion of news and current affairs has a direct relevance to the formation of social policy. Social and political issues are not confined to news and current affairs programmes, for soap operas and chat shows are often the place where such issues are raised. Television is a ubiquitous technology, most households own one main set and many have portables which can be viewed in other rooms. The flickering screen is an increasing presence: life can revolve around the television with meals often eaten in front of it, whether this be the kitchen portable or on a tray in front of the main set. There is an increasing amount of television: a major expansion in the UK was day-time TV, now we have all-night TV, cable and satellite television. Cable and satellite TV have produced television in abundance: some households in the UK now have more than twenty channels. The video cassette recorder (VCR) has ensured that television output can now be viewed at a time of the viewer's own choosing.

Television relates to most areas of social life: influencing how we think, how we vote, what we buy. It is one of the most popular forms of leisure: on average people in the UK spend twenty-six hours a week watching it. Each day 80 per cent of the population watch TV and 94 per cent watch at some time during the week (Department of

National Heritage, 1992). Indeed, such is the attachment of some
people to television that in a recent opinion poll survey 15 per cent
said that they would refuse to give up their television set even if they
were offered £1 million! (*Independent*, 25.1.93) As a medium it is easy
to watch. There are no 'high entry thresholds': you do not need a
degree to watch TV; for many programmes you do not even need to
be able to read. The audience for the mass media might be said to be
passive: they are informed and entertained and sit and watch and
listen. It is this passivity which, in the past, gave rise to all sorts of
fears about the growth of indolence and moral laxity among the
audience. Nonetheless the television audience does not merely
absorb the content of programmes but has a critical stance towards
the screen's output on the basis of lived experience. To a certain
extent our perceptions of the world are derived from the images
which we receive via the television. Most people rely on television as
their main source of information. In the 1980s the power of television
was demonstrated with the remarkable Band Aid concert which, via
TV, linked pop concerts in three continents and raised millions for
famine relief in Africa. This work continues with children in need and
disability appeals. Television attracts a lot of criticism as a medium
which has accelerated the privatization of life but it has, at times, the
extraordinary power to unite people across the country, and in some
international events, like the Olympics, across the world.

The broadcasting system is now in the throes of a major debate on
public service broadcasting caused by the opportunities presented by
technology in the form of cable and satellite, which have greatly
increased the number of channels potentially available to viewers.
The imminence of digital compression of television signals which will
permit a further significant expansion of the number of channels is
another stimulus to rethinking the concept of public service broadcasting. In this chapter the notion of the public interest in
broadcasting is examined with particular reference to the implications
for minorities and the disadvantaged. The redefinition of public
service broadcasting in a pluralistic world of commercial and state
broadcasting has had as its focus the future of the British Broadcasting Corporation (BBC) as that organization's charter will expire in
1996. This chapter examines the origins of the BBC and commercial
television and reviews the debates between advocates of public
service and choice. The debate on the future of broadcasting has an
important connection with ideas of citizenship, and the chapter
concludes with a discussion of the public interest.

The British Broadcasting Corporation

The BBC began life as a private firm, the British Broadcasting Company, in 1922 but within a few years it was taken over by the government and became a public corporation. Sir John Reith was the first Director General of the BBC and he imposed his version of public service on the Corporation so strongly that it characterized thinking within the corporation long after he had left in 1938. Reith thought that the BBC's responsibility was 'to carry into the greatest possible number of homes everything that is best in every department of human endeavour and achievement' (Blumler, 1992, p. 11). From the beginning the BBC made an especial point of its mission to explain: exemplified in the sculpture of Prospero and Ariel on the front of Broadcasting House in London with the words 'Nation shall speak unto Nation' immediately underneath. Although Reith departed from the BBC shortly before the Second World War his high-minded principles lived on. The BBC was important during the war in solidifying national unity and it assumed a symbolic importance in the lives of millions of people through its news and entertainment programmes. Perhaps the Corporation's finest hours were in the immediate post-war years when it began to develop the television service, and expand its radio services with the new 'highbrow' network the Third Programme (now Radio 3). The Third was essentially a creation of the wartime mood which resulted in the Arts Council and the expansion of adult education – attempts, funded by government, to respond to the demand for serious education and culture.

Commercial Television

By the 1950s the same voices who had called for an end to wartime controls over prices and wages extended their attention to broadcasting. Why was it, they argued, that there was no commercial television in this country? In 1953 the televising of the Coronation of HM Queen Elizabeth the Second demonstrated the power of the medium. To us, more than forty years later, it seems difficult to comprehend but at that time it was extraordinary for the television audience, 'commoners', to have as good a view of the coronation in Westminster Abbey as the Archbishop of Canterbury. The Coronation was a real boost to television set sales: it was estimated that 56 per cent of the population – over 29 million people – had watched the service in

Westminster Abbey, a remarkable figure given that there were only 2,140,000 licences. The BBC broadcast of the event was widely admired for its skilful presentation and it gained considerable prestige as a result. Television had become an affordable medium for large numbers of people by the early 1950s. The number of television sets was now increasing rapidly: in 1951 there were one million but by 1955 there were five million. These were the years when the Conservative government went in for a 'bonfire of controls' ending general restrictions on the economy, and especially on the home consumer market, left over from the war and the austerity years of the immediate post-war period. Consumerism was emerging: there were two and a quarter million cars in 1952 but three and a quarter by 1955 (Briggs, 1985, p. 275). In these auspicious circumstances a commercial television lobby formed.

It was not so much the appeal of commercial television but rather the dissatisfaction with the monopoly status of the BBC which persuaded some influential people to support the idea of an alternative to the corporation. Since its inception in 1926 the BBC has been one of those public bodies which has been pored over every so often – usually once a decade – by a committee of experts. It is as though 'Aunty BBC' has an interesting gynaecological condition requiring her to submit to the probing, prodding, investigations of a committee of experts who then pronounce on her general health. In the late 1940s the Labour government appointed such a committee on the future of broadcasting, and chose W H Beveridge to head the enquiry. This invitation came at the end of a decade in which Beveridge had produced more reports than most public figures manage in a lifetime. The 1942 Social Insurance Report was to ensure that his name would go down in the history books and had made him a war-time celebrity with the British people. Two years later he followed this with the sequel, *Full Employment in a Free Society*, and then in 1948 produced a report on *Voluntary Action*. With all this experience behind him it was no surprise that the committee got to work quickly, meeting within three days of its appointment, and under Beveridge's guidance produced mountains of evidence – the BBC's alone amounted to 640,000 words – and the final report, in two volumes, was published early in 1951 (Briggs, 1985, p. 157). The BBC's evidence argued that to break its monopoly and start an alternative radio and television service financed by advertising would mean 'good, in the long run, will inescapably be driven out by the bad' (Briggs, p. 260). But it was by no means certain that Beveridge would agree with this view – he so distrusted monopolies that at the start of his work he wrote that he was looking out for 'the four scandals of monopoly: bureaucracy, complacency, favouritism and inefficiency' (Curran and Seaton, 1991, p. 190). But in the event the committee were persuaded that the monopoly should remain, with one exception: the future Conservative Chancellor of the Exchequer, Selwyn Lloyd, who in a dissenting minority report called for both commercial television and radio. Yet, as we shall see, within a few years it was Lloyd's view which prevailed. In 1954 the Television Act permitted the introduction of commercial television in the UK and the first transmissions began the following year, although commercial radio did not arrive until 1971. The British public had not been entirely insulated from commercial broadcasting. In the 1930s Radio Luxembourg had started to transmit commercial programmes to England and these acquired large audiences, especially on Sunday nights when the BBC only transmitted religious programmes! Some of the most popular of the Luxembourg programmes were transferred direct to commercial television when it started in 1955.

From Monopoly to Duopoly

The lobby for commercial television included the advertising agency J Walter Thompson and Pye, a major TV set manufacturer. It was not a straightforward matter to get the principle accepted by the Conservative government as there was not a great deal of support within the party. There were fears that the vulgarities of American commercialism would be introduced in this country and these seemed to be confirmed by the American networks' treatment of the Coronation since they could not desist from interspersing it with adverts. The communion service was interrupted by an advert for 'Pepperell's Bed Sheets' and General Motors at another point told viewers that its automobiles were 'America's Crown jewels' and one car was the 'Queen of the Road' (Wilson, 1961, p. 157).

The opposition to commercial television came from a diverse variety of sources. It was not a straight party political issue: it was to be expected that the Labour Party would be opposed to commercial TV but large sections of the Conservative Party were as well. Indeed, it would appear that the British establishment – leaders of the churches, voluntary organizations, university vice-chancellors – were opposed to its introduction, which was promoted by a small group within the Conservative party. A study of the introduction of commercial television concluded that 'Britain was given commercial television against the advice of almost all the nominal leaders of society in education, religion and culture, as well as significant sections of the business community' (Wilson, p. 215). The arguments were chiefly to do with the quality of broadcasting which it was thought that independent television would bring. It was suspected that an appeal would be made to the 'lowest common denominator' in order to attract the mass audience for the advertiser and that less popular programmes would die out, suffocated by their poor audience figures.

The BBC, which had long been hailed as the first example of public service broadcasting in the world, was a model for the new service. An Independent Television Authority was created whose job it was to allocate franchises to regional ITV companies. The companies had two rules: to produce programmes of local interest for their region and to produce programmes for the entire ITV network. The task of the ITA – later the Independent Broadcasting Authority when commercial radio arrived – was to ensure that programmes were of sufficient quality. The advertising which was carried was not in the form of the sponsorship of programmes as with some American television but 'spot' advertising which was limited to six minutes each hour (later increased to seven) and was meant to be a 'natural break', although critics found it hard to see how a 'natural break' could be found in some programmes such as plays or films.

The competition from this new service meant that the BBC had to concentrate more resources on television. The decision to do this had been taken in the early 1950s and within a few years there occurred a switch in the mass audience from the radio to the television. After 1956 the BBC had to battle with ITV for the audience share, as if it fell below 20 per cent, as it threatened to in the late 1950s, then it was doubtful if the government would sanction the collection of the licence fee from 80 per cent of the television viewers for a 20 per cent audience.

The unpopularity of the new commercial service with opinion leaders in the country was underlined with the publication of the Pilkington Report. In 1960 Sir Harry Pilkington, of the St Helen's glass factory, was asked by the government to chair another committee on the future of broadcasting in the UK. The report, published in 1962, was a major endorsement of the BBC's role as a public service broadcasting organization: it gave the go-ahead for the corporation to start a second TV channel (to emerge as BBC 2 in 1964). The 1960s was perhaps the most adventurous decade for the BBC. It introduced satire to the television screen; produced controversial documentaries and socially realistic drama. But for ITV the report was gloomy reading: Pilkington felt that the ITV companies were not doing their job properly – the entertainment programmes they provided were not of sufficiently high standard – and the staff of the companies were not given sufficient room to do their job as professionals. The committee accused the companies of exploiting the working-class audience for profit giving them a diet of shoddy commercialized quiz programmes together with westerns and crime series. To the defence that people did not have to watch these programmes the committee took the view that the choices that working-class people made in their television viewing were not real ones as they had not been offered a full range of choices; furthermore, the choices that the working class could make were limited by their education, wealth and leisure (Curran and Seaton, 1991, p. 109).

Pilkington was part of a debate in the 1960s about the nature, purpose and effects of advertising. The consumer society had emerged in Britain in the 1950s and it was felt by a body of opinion, including many in the Labour Party, that advertising on independent television was its siren voice appealing to base and selfish instincts. Although the Pilkington Committee received plenty of complaints about the nature of adverts and their too frequent occurrence in programmes, a broader criticism was that commercial television was promoting a view of society where materialism was taken for granted. This outright antagonism to commercial television as such is now a small minority view and the opposition to advertising is much more muted. In part this is because of the way in which advertising has entered so many aspects of life, via commercial sponsorship, and the importance given to marketing and public relations by almost every organization, be it public or private.

Both ITV and the BBC were to remain in the same institutional form until Noel Annan was invited to chair another committee on the future of broadcasting. The Annan Report 1977 is a milestone in the history of British broadcasting because in its proposals it broke with the public service tradition which Curran and Seaton have defined as 'catering for all sections of the community, reaching all parts of the country regardless of cost, seeking to educate, inform and improve and prepared to lead public opinion rather than follow it' (p. 297). Instead, Annan argued for a 'market place' of broadcasting where individual viewers would be able to choose from a variety of channels. Annan believed that a second channel should be awarded to ITV but that it should be akin to a publisher, not making its own programmes but broadcasting those made by independent companies – this was the origin of Channel 4. These themes were given another airing by the Peacock Committee appointed by the government in 1986 to consider whether advertising should be permitted on the BBC. The committee rejected this as an option, feeling that there would be insufficient advertising income to sustain four channels. The Peacock Committee report articulated a New Right conception of broadcasting in which the consumer (the viewer) was the best judge of his own interest and, while not totally opposed to public service broadcasting, believed that it had been far too paternalistic in the past (Peacock in Veljanovski, 1989, p. xiii).

From Public Service to Choice

Consumer choice between a variety of channels became a reality when broadcasting became extra-terrestrial. Satellite television arrived as an option in 1989 with Sky television. Just as in earlier generations Radio Luxembourg had been outside the control of British governments, likewise in the 1960s the pirate radio stations, so the new satellite channels were difficult to regulate and control. The duopoly had been broken – there was now another television station. But satellite was only one part of the 1980s expansion of television: the other was cable.

Cable television was both a new and an old development. Cable television had been around since the 1950s, providing a service for those people who lived where the reception from an ordinary aerial was too poor to produce a viewable picture. By the late 1970s there were around 2 million subscribers to this service. In other countries the potential for cable has been shown with the development of local cable television stations providing an independent source of news and entertainment. The development of a new form of cable television in this country was linked to the burgeoning of government interest in the question of how the state could promote the growth of information technology. The government decided in the early 1980s that there was a case for developing cable services further: this should be done by private capital and naturally this would entail an entertainment-led approach with the cable companies being able to relay the services from extra-terrestrial satellites; the government ruled that the new cable enterprises should use fibre optics, as this would enable them to carry a much greater range of channels and to carry a telephone system and ISDN material. A Cable Authority was established in 1985 both to approve the opening of new cable franchises and to supervise the broadcasts of the cable operators (its work has now been absorbed into the Independent Television Commission). New cable systems got off to a slow start as they require a considerable financial outlay in the digging up of streets, but progress in cabling accelerated following the government's decision to allow foreign companies to enter the market (Negrine, 1985; Negrine, 1989; McQuail and Siune, 1986, chapter 5). The claims made by optimists about the democracy-enhancing properties of information technology and telecommunications often refer to the interactive services that it is possible to provide with the new cables. There is, however, very little evidence that anything other than commercial criteria have been used in the development of cable in Britain.

As we saw in chapter 2, Communicating, the government in the early 1980s believed that telecommunications could expand without government money. Other countries have identified cable and fibre optics as national infrastructural priorities and paid for their installation. The British strategy has been to allow the private sector to provide these services if they will undertake the cost of investment. One of the *leitmotifs* of the Conservative government of Mrs Thatcher was deregulation and this applied to broadcasting as well as other sectors of the economy. The Conservatives, believing that the state had too great an influence on broadcasting, advocated free competition with the watchword being choice. To quote the White Paper:

> Change is inevitable. It is also desirable: only through change will the individual be able to exercise the much wider choice which will soon become possible. The Government's aim is to open the doors so that individuals can choose for themselves from a much wider range of programmes and types of broadcasting. (Home Office, 1988, 1.2)

The days of the duopoly are now over. The Broadcasting Act 1990 replaced the Independent Broadcasting Authority with the Independent Television Commission, a new authority designed to have a 'light touch' on broadcasting. But in reality the ideals of public service broadcasting remain – the ITC has a battery of powers to enforce certain standards of quality while the BBC remains in situ, having resisted advertising on Radios 1 and 2, or its funding bases being shifted from the licence fee to subscription TV or 'pay per TV' as it is also known where the viewer pays for television services in advance. But if public service broadcasting means that we are all to have access to every channel then this is obviously a thing of the past. Access to

TV will increasingly depend on ability to pay and it is this which worries so many critics of broadcasting trends.

Access

As the mass media multiply it becomes important to establish how open they are, that is, the extent to which individuals, interests and organizations obtain airtime to explain their viewpoint. Those who have access to the air waves have the potential to influence large numbers of people. The Nazi Party realized the power of radio as a means of mass communication in its early years in the 1930s when they used it to broadcast the speeches of Adolf Hitler. Propaganda was recognized as an important weapon both by the Nazis and the Allies in the Second World War and was further developed and refined during the long years of the Cold War by the Americans and the Russians.

The political parties in Western Europe and the United States of America have long recognised the power of television. In the early days of television in the 1950s it was still possible to be a political leader in the UK and mistrust television. Attlee gave monosyllabic answers to interviewers' questions, Churchill was contemptuous of the new medium while Aneurin Bevan complained that it took the 'poetry' out of politics. Harold Wilson, Labour Prime Minister in the 1960s, was the first political leader to take television seriously (as have all his successors), making it a major part of his communication with the electorate (Seymour-Ure, 1991, p. 173). Nowadays television dictates the way in which campaigns are organized and run. It is the major source of news for most people and a 'good television personality' is now a prerequisite for party leaders. Television has imposed a certain style upon political life. It loves political personalities as they are figures whom viewers can see as representative of their party. This has encouraged the 'presidential' trend in British politics with both national parties concentrating on their national leaders. Mrs Thatcher took enormous pains over her TV image and was aided in this endeavour by marketing men from industry. Her adversary, Neil Kinnock, the Labour leader, was also put through the image-makers' treatment and emerged the other side with a proper 'baldie' haircut. Now it is routine for MPs to have their 'colours done' – to be advised which colours suit their skin tones and choose their clothes accordingly. Television has persuaded parties that good pictures are more important than the content of politicians' speeches.

Because of television's power as a medium governments try very hard to influence what appears on our screens: during the Suez crisis the Prime Minister wanted the BBC to drop its impartial view of the war between Britain and Egypt; since the 1960s successive governments have attempted to influence the BBC and ITV. This is understandable but what is worrying in news and current affairs is that certain perceptions of the world are regarded as the way in which the issues should be perceived. Pressure groups or movements which wish to change these 'ways of seeing' face an uphill battle. In the 1980s the peace movement in Britain persuaded a large section of public opinion that the Conservative government's decision to welcome American Cruise missiles was mistaken and dangerous. CND argued that the Soviet Union was not the threatening superpower – the 'Evil Empire' in President Reagan's words – that some Western commentators talked of. With hindsight, after the collapse of the Soviet Union in 1991, we can see that the Russian threat was greatly exaggerated but CND found itself, in media discussions, forced into pro- or anti-Russian preconceptions.

Political leaders, commercial organizations and business all realize the power of television. But what precisely does this power consist of? Television is a medium which analyses, interprets and explains but above all it entertains. The highest viewing figures are almost always for entertainment programmes. Because it is a visual medium it is adept at explaining pictures and images. But is not so good at explaining complex ideas. It needs pictures or rather programme makers think that we, the audience, need pictures, to make sense of the world. 'Talking Heads' are regarded as a turn-off by many programme makers.

Advertisers are another group with a major interest in influencing what appears on our screens. Images are powerful and seductive on television. This is why major firms have such large advertising budgets, but how beneficial is this for our society as opposed to the advertisers? Every hour on British commercial television there are seven minutes' advertising devoted to extolling the merits of a range of products. What effect does this have on the viewing and buying public? The conventional wisdom has been that good advertising cannot sell a bad product, although clearly a lot of advertising does work or firms would not pay such large sums for it. Apart from the question as to whether advertising actually does work – in the sense that it sells goods – it can be said to endorse a certain world view. This is materialistic and consumer-goods oriented, pushing powerful messages which seem to say 'you too can be attractive, powerful,

sexy if you use this product'. Stuart Hood has described the influence
of advertising on the developing world:

> Television programmes are their vanguards. They serve a dual purpose
> . . . they create in politically and economically independent countries a
> concept of a lifestyle that can – if only in part symbolically – be captured
> by purchasing the products advertised on the screen and they inculcate
> by constant exposure a western view of the world, of society and of
> human relationships. (1983, p. 94)

This observation is especially pertinent now that the satellite TV
station Star TV based in Hong Kong beams its American soaps and
MTV into the People's Republic of China. In our society there are
grounds for worrying that the cumulative effect of advertising, the
drip-drip of continual promotion of certain life styles – those of able-
bodied, affluent people – will have an effect on the values of our
society. Peter Townsend has argued that the rich promote a certain
style of life which then filters down to the rest of us: 'The rich are not
only favoured by the system and exploit it. They actively shape its
standards or values. They set fashions which become the styles
sought after by the mass of the population' (1979, p. 367). This
promotes a culture of wanting and dissatisfaction in which the
consumer good is regarded as the object which will give us
happiness. Advertising is largely about the creation of a mood, a style
which the viewers are encouraged to identify with – very few adverts
give much information about their product. Whole categories of
people seldom appear in adverts – disabled people, older people
rarely, black people only occasionally. Clearly society will want to be
able to ensure that its own values are not compromised by
advertising: cigarette adverts have been banned and many urge that
alcohol commercials should also disappear from our screens. The
millions put into the promotion of these two products, which have
such obviously deleterious effects on the health of individuals, make
the health promotion and education budgets of the NHS look
derisory. The Pilkington-inspired debate about the role of advertising
took place in a country where advertising was far less pervasive than
it is today. It is very difficult to get away from advertising: on the
buses, or in the queue at the post office there are video adverts.
Sponsorship of sporting and cultural events by firms is an effective
way of gaining prestige and advertising the company name: by 1986
nearly 1,600 companies in the UK were sponsoring sport to the total
value of £129 million (Clark, 1988, p. 527). Television of course has a

direct relationship to sponsorship because many events, most of the sporting events, are sponsored in order that this will give free television advertising for the firm concerned.

Deregulation

The debate about the relative merits of Public Service Broadcasting and commercial broadcasting is partly about access. The BBC and ITC have, in their charters, a duty to produce programmes for minorities. The fear of the exponents of Public Service Broadcasting is that if it is replaced by commercial television then minority interests will lose out. The proponents of deregulation argue that monopolies or duopolies were appropriate for an earlier technological world in which there was only a small number of channels because there was a finite limit on how many could be allocated. Now with direct broadcasting satellites and cable many more interests can start their own television stations and this includes minorities. The Conservative government's broadcasting policy document, *Broadcasting in the '90s*, reflected the consumer sovereignty argument as it laid a strong emphasis on the viewer making choices and having a greater choice because of the proliferation of new channels (Home Office, 1988). Deregulation has been seen as the most appropriate way to respond to the new technologies. But the White Paper does still provide for the ITC to have a 'light touch' regulatory role. Clearly some economic liberals would want an absence of controls on what could be said or done on television. Yet even on Cable TV in the USA, which has fewer restrictions than most television systems, Manhattan Cable, with its full-frontal sex shows, can only show cream being licked from a girl's nipple and not her vagina.

The free-market viewpoint is espoused by Rupert Murdoch, the media magnate. 'Market-led media ensure competition. Competition lets individual consumers decide what they want to buy. It keeps prices low and quality high . . .' (Keane, 1991, p. 53). The duopoly in Britain has been criticized for raising production costs to excessive heights because of the fact that there are no other players in the TV market than BBC/ITV (p. 55). Technical staff were able to inflate their salaries because of the absence of competition. In addition, the advertising fees are too high. The paternalism of state media is no longer appropriate. The BBC have talked down to the British public for too long. Lord Reith, 6ft 5ins tall, insisted at the inception of the BBC that 'there should be no concessions to the vulgar'. He wrote: 'it is occasionally indicated to us that we are apparently setting out to give the public what we think they need and not what they want, but few know what they want, and very few what they need . . . In any case it is better to overestimate the mentality of the public than to underestimate it' (Briggs, p. 55). Murdoch claimed that these Reithian assumptions still persisted into the world of television: 'the assumption that the people could not be trusted to watch what they wanted to watch, so that it had to be controlled by like-minded people who knew what was good for us' (quoted in Keane, p. 57).

Among the opponents of deregulation are those who forecast that the likely pattern of events will be large media corporations, like Rupert Murdoch's News International, moving in and taking over much of the programming. They instance the present concentration of media power by conglomerates:

> by the beginning of the 1980s most major American media – newspapers, magazines, radio, television, books and movies – were controlled by fifty corporations. Twenty corporations control more than half the 621 million daily newspapers sold every day; twenty corporations control more than half the revenues of the country's 11,000 magazines; three corporations control most of the revenues and audience in television; ten corporations in radio, eleven corporations in all kinds of books; and four corporations in the motion pictures. (Bagdikian quoted by Carl Sessions Stepp in Lichtenberg, 1990, p. 189)

Deregulation enables these multinational media corporations to sell products from different parts of their empire. The media division can produce a TV series based on a book from the publishing division while the music division can market the theme music. This is what they call an attractive synergy, or combined action.

Pay-Per View

The new forms of television which are becoming available differ from the old television channels in that they have an entry price: for satellite broadcasting the cost of the dish and a monthly rental, for cable television the connection charge and a monthly rental. In both services the rental fee gives access to a basic range of channels but there are additional charges for the other channels which show recent cinema films. What has been created is a two tier television service: the terrestrial channels for the majority of the population and the additional channels for cable and satellite viewers. In the case of cable it will be uneconomic to lay the cables in remote and outlying parts of the country, denying their inhabitants the chance to see these programmes. One of the definitions of the public interest in broadcasting was that national events should be covered by television so that it would be open to all to watch them. Arguably some British football matches are a national event but they will not be available to all now that they are only broadcast in their entirety to those who receive Sky via cable or satellite.

We are at the beginning of a process which can be characterized as the transition from citizenship to consumerism in broadcasting: the BBC and ITV duopoly ensured that all parts of the country were covered by their services but the new subscription services appeal to viewers as consumers in a media market where the better off can obtain more channels than others and the poor and the low paid find it difficult to gain entry at all. As we have seen in the case of football, it can also mean that the public services are priced out of certain markets with the result that the range of coverage presented is less than it was (see Golding and Murdock, 1986; Murdock and Golding, 1989; Golding and Murdock, 1989; Golding, 1990). The £15 a month or more which it costs on average to be a cable TV subscriber is beyond the reach of many people in this country, or they might decide that television was so important to their household that they paid the fee and as a result had less to spend on necessities such as food and clothing. This sum each month clearly represents a larger percentage of income to someone on the national average wage than to a highly paid person. In table 3.1 the Family Expenditure Survey demonstrates the way in which spending on media services increases by income size of household.

The experience in other countries is that the overall quality of programmes suffers with the onset of deregulation. In the United States in the 1980s there was a proliferation of TV including VCRs and satellite and in the 1990s more than 60 per cent of American households have cable TV. Most Americans can now receive at least fifteen channels and on average they watch six hours a day of TV. This has meant that the audience share of the major networks in prime time declined from 85 per cent in 1980 to 68 per cent in 1988 (Blumler, in Curran and Gurevitch, 1991, p. 194). The multiplicity of channels has given rise to channel hopping and the American viewer 'incessantly grazes across the dial in search of ever more entrancing viewing pastures' (p. 198). In the American system of television popular entertainment programmes are at a premium: because

Table 3.1 Ownership of communication goods among households (1990)

Household income	Television	Telephone	Video Recorder	Home Computer
Under £60	93.7	61.4	13.8	1.0
£ 60 and under £80	95.7	69.8	26.9	3.1
£ 80 and under £100	99.0	76.1	29.8	3.2
£100 and under £125	97.4	80.4	39.0	4.7
£125 and under £150	98.0	87.5	41.1	5.5
£150 and under £175	97.4	78.8	44.0	8.5
£175 and under £225	98.2	85.4	59.2	11.3
£225 and under £275	99.0	94.9	74.3	22.3
£275 and under £325	99.4	95.8	80.8	27.3
£325 and under £375	99.0	94.9	74.3	22.3
£375 and under £425	98.5	97.9	83.6	27.2
£425 and under £475	98.7	96.9	79.5	28.6
£475 and under £550	98.5	97.9	83.6	27.2
£550 and under £650	99.2	99.0	83.0	28.8
£650 and under £800	99.4	98.7	86.8	33.8
£800 or more	99.7	98.9	87.6	34.8

Source: Family Expenditure Survey 1990, table 3, Household Characteristics.

channels are almost all advert-financed, they need to find the biggest audiences. Commercial considerations are paramount, with the network bosses fighting each other for a larger share of a declining market. This means that the American TV diet is an endless round of banal quiz shows, soap operas, games, mini-series and cartoons. The large number of channels does not therefore mean that more variety and diversity is reflected in the programmes because each network is aiming for the largest audience, which means the lowest common denominator. A Public Broadcasting Channel exists where serious drama, current affairs and documentaries are given pride of place in prime time. It carries advertising but has considerable problems in financing itself and would not exist without the support of charitable foundations. Its precarious position might be seen as a warning of what might ensue in a deregulated market-place approach to broadcasting in the UK.

There are a variety of responses from opponents of deregulation but all of them involve the concept of the public interest and a discussion of the meaning of public service broadcasting in the new world of media abundance. Public service broadcasting has provided a universal service for all age groups, catered for as many minorities as possible and done its best to educate and inform. The following definition outlines the large scope of the concept, which according to the Broadcasting Research Unit consists of eight main principles:

1 Universality of appeal: programmes should cater for all interests and
   tastes.
2 Universality of coverage: one main institution should be directly funded
   by the viewers.
3 Broadcasting should be structured in order to encourage competition in
   good programming rather than competition for numbers.
4 Broadcasting should be distanced from all vested interests, and particularly from the government of the day.
5 Broadcasters should recognize their special relationship to the sense of
   national identity and community.
6 Minorities should receive particular provision, especially the disadvantaged.
7 Public guide-lines for broadcasters should be designed to liberate rather
   than restrict the programme makers.
8 Universality of payment. One main institution should be directly funded
   by the users. (Morrison, 1986, p. 13)

The word that recurs the most in this definition is universality. Once
more there are parallels with the National Health Service. Both aim
for national coverage and are concerned with provision for the entire
population. This is not surprising as the creation of the BBC in the
1920s set the pattern for the public corporations which were to
emerge in the next twenty-five years in the UK, including the NHS
along with the National Coal Board, the Central Electricity Generating Board and other public utilities. When radio broadcasting began
in the UK in the 1920s it was thought that here was a case of a natural
monopoly as the wavelengths were in such short supply (Hood in
Golding, Murdock and Schlesinger (eds), 1986, pp. 56–7). Subsequently it has been difficult for the notion of public service
broadcasting to be separated from the role of the BBC. At times it has
seemed as though it could be defined as whatever the BBC chose to
do. But as we have seen, the mid-1950s saw the launch of commercial
television which was also bound by the public service model. The
regulation of the ITV companies was carried out by the Independent
Television Authority whose remit was to ensure that programmes
reflected certain criteria: balanced programming, a high quality in the
production of programmes and a balance between types of programme.

   Television and radio have themselves changed the nature of public
life. It is now recognized that the public have a right to be informed
about the policies of government and television has a duty to quiz
ministers about government policies. This was not granted without a
struggle: in the 1950s television and radio were still bound by the
fourteen-day rule which stopped them from discussing any matter

which would be debated in Parliament in the next fortnight. Scannell (1989) has argued that televison has produced a new kind of public life by broadcasting sporting and other national events which give every viewer a chance to see national events. The Coronation of Queen Elizabeth the Second in 1953 might be said to be the first of these national events mediated through TV. Another change lies in the presentation of social problems: it was innovatory and daring for broadcasters in the 1930s to get people in poverty or with other problems to talk directly to camera yet now in documentaries this is commonplace. Television, through its relentless diet of soaps and serials, does give a culture in common which provides a source of conversation, if nothing else, for all manner of people (Scannell, 1989).

In the new world of media abundance some claim that we need less, not more, television. Just as motor-cars used to be seen as neutral vehicles for travelling around and are now seen by many people as harmful because of road deaths, environmental pollution and dislocation of communities by new roads, so there are now some who see television as responsible for some of our contemporary woes. Television is blamed for inducing too much passivity in its audience, creating a nation of couch potatoes. The medium is blamed for encouraging an interest in the easy and the superficial. This is an argument which is made particularly in relation to children who watch in the UK an average of three hours a day (Gunter and McAleer, 1990, p. 13). Critics argue that children will naturally watch the 'easiest' TV programmes and not the most informative, and are given a superficial account of the world which they find it hard to assimilate. Postman goes so far as to argue that television is leading to the disappearance of childhood. He believes that from an early age children are presented with an adult view of the world and not a child's view so that they are forced into a premature maturity (1983). The attention span of children is reduced, making them less capable of absorbing information over a long period. Television operates in short bursts of information – three minutes at most – while school teachers might expect their class to concentrate for ten times as long. In a later book, *Amusing Ourselves to Death* (1986), Postman puts forward a similar thesis about the debilitating impact of American television on American public life. He is particularly critical of the way that TV handles news and current affairs where personalities, sound bites, advertising and PR get in the way of serious discussion of issues. There is a convincing argument to be made that the leisure hours of many people in Britain could be devoted to more active pursuits than watching the television. Nicholas Garnham argues, not for the elimination of television, but its containment, viz. that it should not be allowed to expand any more than it has. Garnham is worried about the consequences for quality if media proliferation goes ahead: the consensus that there should be more channels and that these would represent the increasing diversity of our society is wrong-headed. He feels that the socialist movement in Britain has been 'infected' by the ideology of choice popular in advanced industrial societies and that any expansion should be of the public sector, because it is only through the public sector that a democratic culture can be sustained (Garnham, 1990, p. 133).

Citizenship is being promoted as an integrative principle for social policy in the late twentieth century, but in order to exercise citizenship rights properly a certain degree of political knowledge is required. Yet studies of the political literacy of the UK population reveal a depressing picture of ignorance about political institutions. In this sense television has failed, as for all its power it has not produced a sophisticated electorate. Indeed, it might be argued that television has been responsible for a trivialization of politics, with a preference for image over ideas and style over substance. In order to vote intelligently – and voting is the limit of political participation for most citizens today – people need access to information which can then be used by them to weigh up the claims of politicians.

The technology now exists for every city and small town to have its own radio and television stations, unlike the past when broadcasting systems had to operate within a world of scarcity as wavelengths were strictly allocated to countries and could only be increased with international agreement. But the content of the transmissions is more problematic. Should the stations operate on a purely commercial basis or should they operate with a commitment to public service broadcasting? Both kinds of station operate in most places. There is a sense in which local issues go unreported by the modern media. Council debates are not generally broadcast by local radio stations in their entirety. Local newspapers often offer only a very selective report of what was said in the council chamber or in the council committee. Yet this is after the passage of legislation which has enabled the public to be able to attend both committees and full council meetings. Those who represent the public, in this case the local journalists, deem that it would not be of interest to their listeners or their readers for them to be given the full debate but instead they must be content with soundbites or short paragraphs. Despite this extremely selective broadcasting and reporting, local government operates with a concept of accountability to elected representatives and through them to the public. It needs to be said that this selective coverage was not always the case. One hundred years ago, when male democracy was young, many local newspapers were papers of record: they reported what was said in the council chamber almost verbatim; the same could be said of their coverage of public and political meetings. There can be few local newspapers who can now hold themselves up as papers of record with any justification. The radio station and the cable television studio are the late twentieth-century equivalent of the public meeting and Speakers Corner: they are the market-place of democracy, where people can come together as *citizens* and debate their common problems. As such there is a major responsibility on them to cater for the range of opinions which are now to be found in this country. The health of our broadcasting media is a matter of some importance for the functioning of a healthy democracy. There are good grounds for concern. There is the paradox that the level of political illiteracy is high yet the means to educate and inform people have never been better. Social policy suffers from this deficit of knowledge and understanding among the general public, in the way that most discussions of policy do not really enter the public realm in an unfinished format, rather they are released as government packages which are to be debated and commented upon but not expected to be unpacked, altered or shaped by public opinion.

It is at this point that the optimists whom we met in chapter 2 come forward arguing that cable TV will be a means of producing 'teledemocracy': a society in which there can be direct democracy, with referenda on all issues because people will be able to vote from the comfort of their armchair. But as Arterton has pointed out, 'any mechanism of communication that costs money to use will necessarily produce inequalities of access among social and economic groups. When these media become conveyors of political participation, differential access, both as to speakers and listeners, can become unduly restrictive from the viewpoint of a democracy' (quoted in Ferguson, 1990, p. 93). In the British context, where it is commercial considerations and interests alone which are funding the expansion of cable, their plans in building in opportunities for feedback from homes to a central point are non-existent.

One ought as well to be able to 'recommunicate' through the media as well as receive communication, but when television programmers aim to attract the largest audience this is unlikely. The importance of this is in part a question of numbers. A poor viewing figure for a programme is 750,000 while a very good figure is 20 million, but then compare this low figure with the average sales figure for a hardback book (5,000 copies), or the sales of a political weekly, say, twenty to thirty thousand. This difference in magnitude is in part what is meant when the term 'mass media' is employed. It is said that the right and the ability to communicate are an essential component of citizenship. For this purpose it is essential that the media inform and involve people in the political process.

There is then an obvious scepticism about many of the optimistic scenarios which posit a more engaged and informed democracy as a result of technological developments. Rather it could be said that we will only get these technological developments as a by-product of an informed democracy. Voters will need to be more involved in the process of local and national politics in order to see the value of referenda at the push of a television button on a major local issue. But how much do voters know about politics? The answer is – alarmingly – very little. Access is an important word in this discussion. Interpreted in one way access is about the range of views that are presented on television. More broadly, it can refer to the ability of households to use communication media. We are moving from an era in which the duopoly of BBC and ITV ensured that services were universally available – to those who paid a licence fee – to one where the entry point will be ability to pay. The poor 'are priced out of the markets for new services and left with an infrastructure of public provision that is either unable or unwilling to provide the full range of resources for citizenship' (Murdock and Golding, 1989, p. 184).

There is now a view which says that we are a society so variegated, multi-cultural and pluralist that the public broadcasting services cannot capture this diversity. Writers of this persuasion (Keane, 1991; Mulgan, 1991) argue that public corporations like the BBC must be abandoned as the embodiment of public service broadcasting. That does not mean that we abandon the concept, just the institutions. In their place, the state regulates the private broadcasting sector by insisting on access for minorities and public debates, and guarantees that work by independent producers is broadcast. Further, a strict legal framework is introduced which ensures that minimum standards are complied with. The large media conglomerates would be required to carry messages and views of citizen groups (Keane, pp. 115ff).

Television has had a direct influence on Social Policy through its presentation of social problems. The 1967 play 'Cathy Come Home' was a hard-hitting account of the impact of homelessness on a young mother. Its shock impact led to homelessness moving up the agenda of public debate and greatly increased support for Shelter, the housing charity. Subsequently other programmes have been as successful in focusing public attention on a single issue. The public service duopoly has produced a stream of good programmes on social policy and social problems. There is concern that this will not be the case if the notion of the public interest is allowed to decline.

This is not to say that those who are major users of health and social services see their views and interests accurately represented on television. While the specialist programmes are of a high quality and reflect the concerns of minorities it is the portrayal of people in the rest of the television output which is more problematic. Disabled people are under-represented in British television. A recent survey revealed that they accounted for only 1.4 per cent of all the characters portrayed although they amount to 14 per cent of the adult population (Cumberbatch and Negrine, 1992, p. 136). The study found that disabled people tend to be represented through stereotypes, the criminal or a pathetic, powerless person. On the whole they are low status people: 'Further, disabled characters were far more likely than their able-bodied compatriots to be either aggressive or the victims of violence, and they were more than three times as likely as able-bodied characters to be dead by the end of the programme' (p. 138).

A study of press coverage of disability has shown that the medical problems of disabled people predominate to the virtual exclusion of their political and social status, with issues relating to mobility receiving the least attention of all despite its obvious importance for them (Smith and Jordan, 1991, p. 22). The same concentration of stereotypes has been found to operate in the case of elderly people, with unfavourable images in the ascendant. This is particularly unfair as audience research has revealed that older people are the most committed part of the audience (Dant and Johnson 1991; Midwinter, 1991).

Public *interests* is a more appropriate way of thinking about broadcasting policy, for we now live in a society characterized by diversity. The new media enable this diversity to flourish and be represented. The days of scarcity in broadcasting are over: even if the British government were to set its face resolutely against any more channels the introduction of cable and satellite would ensure that the British public had a much wider choice of programmes. The multiplicity of channels means that a much greater range of audiences can be catered for but the commercial considerations which drive much of this development ensure that this will not be the case, for advertisers require a certain level of audience. Diversity should not be allowed to become mere fragmentation in which it is impossible to achieve a national debate in the society. If this were to occur then the production of Social policy becomes that much more difficult for it has no common assumptions to build upon or appeal to. The media abundance of the 1990s should not mean that users of social services are confined to specialist programmes. If citizenship is to have a meaning then the media need to retain their important role as the forum in which we talk to each other and discuss and debate the concerns of our time.

Discussion Questions

1 Is the regulation of broadcasting beyond the control of the nation state?
2 Is there still a place for public service broadcasting in the 1990s?

Further Reading

James Curran and Jean Seaton, *Power without Responsibility: the Press and Broadcasting in Britain* (4th edn, Routledge, 1991) is a key reference; especially relevant is chapter 17 on public service broadcasting. John Keane, *The Media and Democracy* (Polity Press, 1991) is an argument for the redefinition of public service broadcasting. Cento Veljanovski (ed.), *Freedom in Broadcasting* (Institute of Economic Affairs, 1989), is a stimulating collection of essays by Alan Peacock and Samuel Brittan and others arguing for the primacy of the market in broadcasting. Colin Seymour-Ure, *The British Press and Broadcasting since 1945* (Blackwell, 1991) is a good concise account.

References

BBC (1992), *Extending Choice: the BBC's role in the new broadcasting age*.
Blumler, J G (1992), *Television and the Public Interest: Vulnerable Values in West European Broadcasting*, London: Sage.
Briggs, A (1985), *The BBC: the first fifty years*, Oxford: Oxford University Press.
Clark, E (1988), *The Want Makers*, London: Coronet.
Cumberbatch, G and Negrine, R (1992), *Images of Disability on Television*, London: Routledge.
Curran, J and Gurevitch, M (eds) (1991), *Mass Media and Society*, London: Edward Arnold.

Curran, J and Seaton, J (1991), *Power without Responsibility: the press and broadcasting in Britain*, 4th edn, London: Routledge.

Dant, T and Johnson, M (1991), 'Growing old in the eyes of the media', in B Franklin and N Parton (eds), *Social Work, the Media and Public Relations*, London: Routledge.

Department of National Heritage (1992), *The Future of the BBC*, London: HMSO.

Ferguson, M (ed.) (1990), *Public Communication: the new imperatives*, London: Sage.

Garnham, N (1990), *Capitalism and Communication*, London: Sage.

Golding, P (1990), 'Political communication and citizenship: the media and democracy in an inegalitarian social order', in M Ferguson (ed.), *Public Communication: the new imperatives*, London: Sage.

Golding, P and Murdock, G (1986), 'Unequal information: access and exclusion in the new communications market place', in M Ferguson (ed), *New Communications Technologies and the Public Interest*, London: Sage.

Golding, P and Murdock, G (1989), 'Pulling the plugs on democracy', *New Statesman and Society*, 30 June.

Golding, P, Murdock, G and Schlesinger, P (eds) (1986), *Communicating Politics: mass communications and the political process*, Leicester: Leicester University Press, 1986.

Gunter B and McAleer, J (1990), *Children and Television: the one-eyed monster*, London: Routledge.

Home Office (1988), *Broadcasting in the '90s: competition, choice and quality*, London: HMSO.

Hood, S (1983), *On Television*, 2nd edn, London: Pluto Press.

Keane, J (1991), *The Media and Democracy*, Oxford: Basil Blackwell.

Lichtenberg, J (1990), *Democracy and the Mass Media*, Cambridge: Cambridge University Press.

McQuail, D (1992), *Media Performance: mass communication and the public interest*, London: Sage.

McQuail, D and Siune, K (eds) (1986), *New Media Politics: comparative perspectives in Western Europe*, London: Sage.

Midwinter, E (1991), *Out of Focus: old age, the press and broadcasting*, London: Centre for Policy on Ageing.

Morrison, D (1986), *Invisible Citizens*, London: Broadcasting Research Unit.

Mulgan, G (1991), *The Question of Quality*, London: British Film Institute.

Murdock, G and Golding, P (1989), 'Information Poverty and Political Inequality: citizenship in the age of privatised communications', *Journal of Communication*, 39, 3 (summer), 180–95.

Negrine, R (1985), 'Cable television in Great Britain', in R Negrine (ed.), *Cable Television and the Future of Broadcasting*, London: Croom Helm.

Negrine, R (1989), *Politics and the Mass Media in Britain*, London: Routledge.

Postman, N (1983), *The Disappearance of Childhood*, London: W H Allen.

Postman, N (1986), *Amusing Ourselves to Death*, London: Heinemann.

Scannell, P (1989), 'Public service broadcasting and modern public life', *Media, Culture and Society*, 11, 135–66.

Seymour-Ure, C (1991), *The British Press and Broadcasting since 1945*, Oxford: Basil Blackwell.

Smith, S and Jordan, A (1991), *What the Papers Say and Don't Say about Disability*, London: The Spastics Society.

Townsend, P (1979), *Poverty in the United Kingdom*, Harmondsworth: Penguin.

Veljanovski, C (1989), *Freedom in Broadcasting*, London: Institute of Economic Affairs.

Wilson, H H (1961), *Pressure Group: the campaign for commercial television*, London: Secker and Warburg.

4

TRAVELLING

In our modern world travelling is accepted as part of daily life. Many of us undertake journeys each day to get to work that in previous centuries would have been a rare occurrence, if contemplated at all. One might almost say that travel has become part of our twentieth-century human condition: from childhood play with toy cars through bicycles, perhaps a mountain bike and then the first car. Often when we have a break from work and go on holiday, we travel. Not being able to get around, to be restricted to a particular place, to be dependent on other people for travel is often a characteristic of disability or imprisonment. Travel has become a major activity in the advanced industrial societies in the twentieth century: the motor car has produced a vast increase in personal travel while the plane has greatly expanded international travel. An average of 1.1 million people are travelling outside their home country everyday – an annual total of 405 million people (Stancliffe, 1992).

The dominant image of transport in our society is individual – 'have you got transport?' means 'do you have a car?' Cars are symbols of an individual's identity and motor manufacturers sell their cars on the promise of speed, performance and style. Public transport in contrast has a downmarket image and in the UK attracts a declining share of the travelling public. Transport can be dangerous, particularly for pedestrians who suffer the highest rates of fatalities and serious accidents. These casualties of our roads are not widely remarked upon although they are more numerous than the numbers involved in air plane disasters. In a curious way we seem as a society to have learnt to live with the deaths arising from Road Traffic Accidents, accepting them as a regrettable consequence of our transport policy.

In the United Kingdom we are confronted by a series of inter-related problems which arise from our transport system. These include traffic congestion, the pollution caused by road transport and the damage to our countryside inflicted by new road building. Although these are all important issues, in this chapter we will be addressing the socioeconomic consequences of the way in which transport is organized in our society. These can often be overlooked but can have an important impact on people's lives, generating new inequalities and reinforcing existing divisions. We will look at the different forms of transport; the impact of our transport system on the urban environment; the needs of the 'transport disadvantaged'; the health costs of the transport system and finally the aims of our transport policy.

Transport in this country is organized on a mixed-economy basis, that is, there is a public and a private sector. British Rail is the major public sector transport operator and the rest of transport provision is now in the private sector. Across the range of government policy since 1979 Conservative governments believed that market forces should play a much greater part in the provision of services which had previously been run by government agencies. Where possible this has led to nationalized industries being sold off to private shareholders as with British Gas, British Telecom and the Electricity Boards. In other sectors some parts of a service have been 'hived off' to the private sector, and this has happened with British Rail.

In 1979 when Mrs Thatcher's radical Conservative government came to power British Rail was obviously vulnerable to a government intent on cutting back the public sector and thereby reducing the public sector borrowing requirement. In 1981 the profitable Sealink ferry services and the British Transport hotels were sold to the private sector. Since that time British Rail has not found the government sympathetic to its arguments that more government money should be provided for modernization plans – to electrify the main lines, to build new trains and to renew track. Britain has an extensive railway system but large parts of it are outdated and British Rail needs money for this purpose. The government's response has been to argue that additional revenue should be raised from fare increases and joint ventures with the private sector (Bagwell, 1984). Although the government was persuaded that the Channel Tunnel should be a rail link, funds have not been forthcoming for a High Speed Link from the Channel Tunnel to major British cities, unlike France where major cities will be connected to the Tunnel. In 1992 the government announced that it intended to privatize parts of British Rail, starting with the profitable Inter-City service. But any company would also face possible competition from other firms allowed to run trains on the track. Various local authorities are investigating the potential of light railways to reduce trafic congestion in the cities. The first scheme of this kind is the Manchester Light Rail scheme which runs partly on BR track and partly on new tram lines built by the Manchester Passenger Transport Authority.

Buses

Buses were the other part of 'public transport' until 1985 when the government transferred them substantially to the private sector. On coming to office the Thatcher government took the view that the bus services, which had mainly become part of the National Bus Company, were not exploiting demand to the full. 'Deregulation' was put forward as the answer – whereby new operators could compete with existing bus companies. The intention was that services would improve as competition forced operators to offer more frequent services. There has been more competition but the evidence for an improved service is hard to find.

The operation and organization of bus services has responded to the changing political climate of public services. In the late nineteenth century the predecessor of the motorbus, the electric tram, was at first in private hands but many cities 'municipalized' their tramways, bringing them under the control of the city council. The advantages were that there was just one operator who could run regular services and for the workers – the tramway men – it was easier to improve their conditions as the employer was open to political persuasion, being ultimately responsible to the ballot box at the local government elections. When motor buses began to replace the trams shortly before and after the First World War the same pattern obtained although there were private operators in many towns and in the country districts. In the inter-war period price controls on bus fares were introduced by the central government in 1930, which made it much more difficult for other private operators to start bus services although private operators continued in existence.

Buses were a buoyant part of the transport system until the 1950s. But after this time, as more households acquired motor cars so the number of passengers on bus routes fell. A spiral of decline had begun. In order to compensate for the fall in the number of passengers the companies raised fares and this in its turn made bus travel less attractive. From the 1950s millions of people acquired their first car and enjoyed the independence that the car can give its driver. Once a person buys a car they rarely make use of public transport.

The government's belief was that irrespective of these disadvantages in relation to other forms of transport the bus operators were not keeping pace with the changed travel needs of the population and they felt that private competition would stimulate them to do this. By 1979 the various municipal and private bus operators had been nationalized and formed part of the National Bus Company (NBC). In the 1980 Transport Act the government introduced the possibility of private competition with the National Bus company on routes over thirty miles, and this set off a battle between the NBC and private coach operators which resulted in very low prices, and various services never previously provided on long distance coaches – videos, drinks, toilets. But the government was still not satisfied that there was enough competition: insufficient new bus operators had started on the smaller routes. As a result it introduced the Transport Act 1985, the most comprehensive measure in transport planning for over forty years. It 'deregulated' the buses which meant the previous edifice of controls over service quality, price and operators was removed and the bus companies which formed the NBC were denationalized and sold off to the private sector. Now new operators could start on routes provided they satisfied the local transport authority on a number of minor conditions. Numerous companies started to compete with the existing bus providers. Because they were in business to make a profit they started services on the most popular routes where they could be assured of a regular supply of passengers. The travellers on these routes saw the number of services increase. But another effect of the 1985 Transport Act was that subsidies for uneconomic routes which were run because they fulfilled a social need were reduced although councils still had funds for the subsidy of uneconomic routes. The pattern of bus operators saw a number of changes: some companies were subject to management buy-outs, whilst there were many amalgamations. Five years later the small, newly created companies had mostly been taken over by two large companies. In effect, the monopoly which the Transport Act 1985 had broken up in the public sector had become a private sector duopoly.

The most obvious form of transport – using one's own legs – tends to be neglected in many official discussions of transport. Yet one journey per person per day is made on foot and more than one in three of all journeys that people make are walking journeys (Hillman, cited in Whitelegg, 1988). A study conducted at the end of the 1970s concluded that over 48 million journeys a year were made on foot (Hillman and Whalley, 1979). As can be seen from the list below walking is the most popular mode for short journeys, that is under one mile:

Percentage of journeys under one mile according to transport mode

Walk	84
Bicycle	2
Motorcycle	–
Car driver	7
Car passenger	5
Van/lorry	–
Local bus	1
Coach/express bus	0
Train	–
Other	0
Total	100 (Potter and Hughes, 1990, p. 14, Table 11.)

For children and young people walking is an obvious transport option. Yet on the evidence of our pavements transport planners seem to be conspiring to make walking difficult. The environment for pedestrians in towns and cities is a poor one. Over the years more and more priority has been given to motorized traffic at the expense of the pedestrian. The classic illustration of this is the phasing out of zebra crossings and their replacement with pelican crossings. Once a pedestrian steps onto a zebra crossing she or he has right of way over the oncoming traffic which has to stop. Yet the pelican crossing only gives the pedestrian right of way when the green man appears. As all pedestrians know this can often take a long time, and the length of time permitted for crossing is often too short for elderly and disabled people and parents with small children. The switch from zebra to pelican was made because planners felt that it was important to keep the traffic moving. Unfortunately many pedestrians cannot be bothered to wait for the lights to change and they jaywalk.

Pavements are not regarded is a major priority by transport planners, indeed, too often they are obstructed by parked cars, advertising boards, sacks of refuse, builder's materials and any number of objects. The problem of cracked and uneven pavements is a common one. Sometimes pavements are just not wide enough for the pedestrians who use them and of course this presents great danger when they are forced off the pavement into the road. Although road accidents are systematically reported pavement accidents are not. A pavement accident, most commonly a fall, can be caused by any number of factors, e.g. slipping on ice, tripping on uneven paving stones or falling over rubbish left on the footpath. The National Consumer Council surveyed this problem in the mid-1980s and found that just one in five of their sample had been involved in a pedestrian accident in the previous year. If these figures were to be grossed up for the entire adult population of the United Kingdom then the numbers requiring medical treatment each year as a result of pavement falls would be about 450,000 (NCC, 1987, p. 33).

Many motorists disregard the rights of pavement users. The motorists who park on the pavement are legion. This presents a hazard to all pedestrians but particularly to children, elderly people, disabled people and the blind. In part this is because of the lack of enforcement of traffic regulations by the police and the shortage of traffic wardens. The position of pedestrians in our transport system is a lowly one – they are frequently disregarded and provision for them is poor. Other road users do not on the whole treat them with any great courtesy or respect. Perhaps this lack of power is related to the kind of people who are pedestrians? As the NCC report points out: 'Walking is of central importance to women rather than men, to those on low incomes rather than to those on high incomes, and to the very young and very old rather than to those of working age' (NCC, p. 3). In other words, the rich, powerful and influential in our society do not use their legs as a major form of transport. Nonetheless we are all pedestrians at one time or another even if is only when we use the pedestrianized shopping centre, walking from the car park to the shops.

There is a growing view that giving a greater priority to pedestrians will enhance city and town life. We are all aware of the noise, pollution and dirt caused by high volumes of motor traffic crawling through urban areas, particularly at rush hours. There has long been a view that pedestrians and cars do not mix. In the Netherlands and Germany there are many traffic restraint zones in residential districts. In Germany they have five key principles described by Whitelegg:

1 Pedestrians may use the entire width of the street, children are allowed to play everywhere.
2 Vehicular traffic must proceed at walking pace.

3 Motorists may neither endanger nor impair pedestrians: they must wait if necessary.
4 Pedestrians may not unnecessarily impair vehicular traffic.
5 Parking outside the specially marked areas is not permitted except for picking up or setting down passengers, loading, or unloading. (Whitelegg, 1988, p. 115)

What the German and Dutch planners recognize is that streets are places, not just thoroughfares for people to travel through. The schemes described here have produced an increase in social contact and neighbourliness as people can begin once more to see the street as part of their living space (Sherlock, 1990).

Of course many of the restrictions on walking as a form of transport which are imposed by the predominance of the motor car also apply to cycling. Cycling is a non-polluting form of transport which is very good physical exercise but hazardous in present-day urban traffic conditions. It will only become a more popular option when the roads are relieved of much of the motorized traffic on them. In the 1980s cycle sales in Britain increased by 80 per cent. More bikes than cars were sold in 1989 (Cyclists Touring Club (CTC), 1991, p. 10). But the number of people who use their bikes is very low: bikes now only account for only 4 per cent of journeys (CTC, p. 2). The potential to increase cycle use is large especially as mountain bikes make cycling in hilly areas less strenuous. If cycle routes were built, separating bikes from cars and other road users, then there is a real possibility that cycling could become much more popular. Journeys to work are an area where cycle use could be increased as a majority of these are less than five miles in length (CTC, p. 12).

Central to the government's philosophy has been a commitment to the freedom of the private motorist. Car ownership greatly increased in the 1980s and the government viewed this as an outcome of increased prosperity. It saw road building as essential to the growth of the economy in the future: personal travel must be facilitated but so too must freight movement by lorries. This stance led the government to announce a major programme of road building in 1989. In the White Paper 'Roads to Prosperity' it was pointed out that since 1980 traffic on the roads had increased by 35 per cent and in the same period the number of vehicles on the roads had increased to over 23 million. The White Paper saw traffic congestion as the central problem: 'Road congestion is bad for the economy. It imposes high costs on industry and other road users, by wasting time, delaying deliveries and reducing reliability, (Department of Transport, 1989, para. 6). As a result the government committed itself to a major road building programme costing £12 billion, described by the then Transport Secretary as 'the largest road programme since the Romans' (Transport 2000, 1990). In its 1989 White Paper the government made two estimates of traffic increase in this country by the year 2025: either an increase of 83 per cent (the low figure) or 142 per cent (the high figure) (Department of Transport, 1989, para. 20).

The Conservative government argued that with a lower rate of car ownership than some other West European countries measures to restrict car ownership would not be warranted. In 1990 the Transport Secretary saw this as a matter of personal freedom: 'Do we tell the one third of families in Britain who do not now own a car that they cannot own one?' (*Guardian*, 1 May 1990). Many Conservatives view the ownership of a car in much the same way as they view home ownership: giving people a stake in the society and encouraging their own initiative. The problem for this school of thought is that traffic forecasts tend to have a self-fulfilling quality, with the new roads that are built to meet the expected increase in traffic actually stimulating more car usage. Car dependency is now an acknowledged feature of our society as shown by the answers given by drivers in a series of opinion surveys in the late 1980s (table 4.1).

It is easy to forget how much of our everyday life is organized

Table 4.1 Degree of dependence on cars reported by drivers in five opinion surveys

I would find it very difficult to adjust my lifestyle to being without a car	Agree 1988 1989	84% 82%
	Disagree 1988 1989	12% 14%
The car is too much part of my lifestyle to consider giving it up	Strongly/Tend to agree	74%
	Strongly/Tend to disagree	21%
A car is essential to our lifestyle, and we would not want to be without one	Agree	69%
A car is not essential to our lifestyle, but we would not want to be without one	Agree	19%
Is having a car an absolute necessity, or could you and your family get along without one if you had to?	Absolute necessity	58%
	Could get along	41%

Source: P Goodwin et al. (1991), table 3.12.

around the use of the motor car. Many children are taken to school in their parent's car. Increasing numbers of students have cars. Large numbers of people use the car to get to work and entertainment, sports and leisure facilities are usually organized with the car in mind. If they are not, like some inner city football stadiums, then they find that there are growing calls for them to be rebuilt on the edge of town. Supermarkets are now relocating to the edge of towns in order that they can provide adequate car parking space for their customers.

Without a car or access to one the quality of your life will be inferior to that of others. You may have to pay more for goods in shops because you will not find it easy to travel to the out-of-town hypermarket in order to obtain lower prices. If you buy a large item it is assumed by many shops that you will have a car to take it home. If an article in your home – the stereo say – breaks down it is assumed that you will be able to bring it along for repair in your car. People live in villages or small towns which are many miles from their place of work. Many people have moved to these areas because they like the idea of living in the countryside but in order to do so they are dependent on their car. Their dependency can be concealed until they are too old to use the car, when they become extremely isolated. Children in rural and semi-rural locations have to be 'ferried' around from home to school, to parties, to their friends. Many journeys are made simply in order to escort children. No other single invention has changed the way in which we live our lives in the twentieth century as much as the motor car.

As is made abundantly clear from innumerable colour magazines and television advertisements, you are what you drive. Motor cars are the products which symbolize the consumer society: they are packaged with reference to their speed, the sexual allure that accompanies a particular make and the emphasis on the individual getting away from society on the wide open roads that only seem to exist in television commercials. The priority given to motor cars has seriously distorted transport policy in this country. But it has also influenced the way in which our social life is organized, and as always the consequences are most detrimental for the poor and disadvantaged. For those who cannot drive or do not have access to a car out of town shopping becomes much more difficult, if not impossible. Many jobs are now barred to people who cannot drive. Various forms of entertainment – theme parks, leisure centres – become very difficult to reach without a motor car. It becomes much harder for the carless to visit friends or relations as bus and train services decline. Many children's activities are denied to those without cars to ferry the children backwards and forwards. Time is consumed by the use of public transport. It can take an hour for one person to travel to work by bus as opposed to another who can get there in fifteen minutes in a car. As the range of activities increases for car owners so social life becomes geographically dispersed and it becomes imperative to own a car.

There are serious social disadvantages which result from present policies which privilege the private car. We have already remarked on how shopping patterns have been altered by the car and out of town shopping seriously disadvantages those who are not mobile. This is a form of deprivation which is as important as those which have been essayed by students of poverty since the turn of the century. Inequalities in transport abound and are connected to wider inequalities. You can be 'transport-rich' or 'transport-poor' in our society. There is mobility deprivation as well as social deprivation. Sutton writes of three levels of mobility choice: Level one is effective demand when one's current mobility needs are satisfied by the available modes of transport; Level two is when mobility is depressed because of an absence of transport or the cost of travel; Level three is frustrated demand when mobility is suppressed to such an extent that travel is not even considered (Sutton, 1988).

Travel to Work

The car has become a much more popular means of getting to work in the last thirty years. In the 1960s our urban buses would be packed at rush hours in the morning or evening with 'standing room only'. Outside of London this is much less common today. In 1972–3 39 per cent of journeys to work by women were made by car whereas in 1985–6 the corresponding figure was 59 per cent. The same trend was, of course, present in journeys made by men. The difference is that men started from a higher percentage of journeys made by car. In 1972–3 61 per cent of all journeys to work made by men were by car – whereas by 1985–6 the car accounted for 72 per cent (see table 4.2).

As can be seen from table 4.2, the bus was the transport mode that lost a significant number of passengers over this same period, particularly among women. In 1972–3 38 per cent of journeys to work by women were made by bus, whereas by 1985–6 this had fallen to 19 per cent. For both sexes journeys by rail remained constant.

Journeys to and from work are often influenced by the employer's policy. A recent report showed that 50 per cent of cars entering

Table 4.2 Transport to and from work

| | Main mode[1] of transport (percentages) | | | | | | | Number of journeys in sample (= 100%) (thousands) |
	Rail	Bus	Car, van, lorry	Motor cycle	Bicycle	Walk[2]	Other	
Females								
1972–3	6	38	39	1	5	8	4	19,622
1975–6	5	30	46	1	6	10	3	32,262
1978–9	4	30	47	1	4	10	4	26,037
1985–6	6	19	59	1	4	7	3	30,925
Males								
1972–3	5	15	61	4	7	5	2	40,171
1975–6	5	11	66	4	7	5	2	61,096
1978–9	4	13	66	3	6	6	2	48,823
1985–6	5	7	72	3	6	4	2	53,269

Source: Social Trends, 1989.
[1] The mode used for the greater part of the journey.
[2] Excludes walks under 1 mile.

London during the rush hour were company cars. The number of company cars, that is cars bought or, more usually, leased by firms has greatly increased in the last thirty years. There were 3.6 million in 1991 (CTC, 1991). Companies give staff cars so that they can use them in the course of their work: the most obvious example is the travelling salesman. But they are often used in lieu of wages for senior executives in a company and are regarded as a 'perk' of the job. They are the most widely available perk for executives and account for two thirds of all new cars sold in the UK (Potter and Hughes, 1990, p. 16), so that they have a significant impact on the car industry. The government encourages this practice by tax concessions on the cost of buying these vehicles, treating them as a 'business expense'. It has been argued that this subsidy to the car industry – the latest estimate is that it is worth £2.8 billion a year – has encouraged motor manufacturers to build vehicles for their high performance and speed rather than their safety and reliability (Guardian, 1 May 1990).

Even if an employee does not have a company car they may well be paid 'mileage' for the use of their own car while on company business. Often this mileage, an amount paid for each mile travelled, is generous and is another inducement to use a car rather than public transport while on company business. Another way in which employers can encourage travel to work by car is by providing free parking at the place of work, an extremely valuable perk in a city like London where parking spaces are so sparse and have to be paid for.

Obviously cars are not only used for transport to and from work. One of their major uses is for social and entertainment purposes: this accounted for 42 per cent of all mileage travelled and 33 per cent of all journeys (*Social Trends*, 1989, table 9.4). For some people cars themselves are a major form of recreation: men especially like to drive around, to enjoy the sensation of movement. But motor car journeys for social and entertainment purposes mean going to visit friends and families or entertainment facilities. As the motor car has become the major form of transport in our society so the entertainment industry has had to accommodate to its requirements. Multiplex cinemas on the outskirts of towns provide sufficient parking space to be viable while inner city cinemas where parking is difficult or expensive lose customers. A great many people engage in Do It Yourself and DIY stores are now usually located on the edge of cities and towns in order to make it easy for car drivers to use them.

Over the last thirty years there has been a transformation of our cities, towns and villages in order to accommodate the car. In 1963 the government-commissioned Buchanan Report outlined two alternative responses to the growth in motor car ownership: a remodelling of our cities and towns to accommodate the car or restrictions on car usage and a big investment in, and promotion of, public transport. Buchanan did not seriously explore the second option and his report is devoted to demonstrating how cities could be replanned and rebuilt around a new road system. In the centres of cities, Buchanan proposed that cars and people be separated and this would be accomplished by having two different levels – roads and pedestrian walkways. There would be 'environmental areas' for family housing and these would be traffic free, being served by a series of distributor roads. There was bipartisan consensus in favour of the Buchanan Report's proposals for rebuilding cities for cars. The Report, described as 'A gigantic effort . . . to replan, reshape and rebuild our cities' (Hill, 1986, p. 91) was very much in line with other movements of the time, for high rise flats, for New Towns, for slum clearance. In his preface to the Buchanan Report Sir Geoffrey Crowther wrote about the problem of traffic congestion, just emerging as the result of increased car ownership, as 'an emergency that is coming upon us' (Buchanan, 1964, p. 5). Almost thirty years later that emergency is with us, but the proposals of Buchanan have not been implemented, nor has there been any other attempt to face the problem.

The growing dominance of the motor car is the outcome of a policy of 'laissez-faire' in transport policy by successive governments. Essentially market forces, which promote car ownership, have been allowed to prevail in the name of individual freedom. Although Labour governments have promoted the public transport sector they have not altered the terms of the battle between private and public transport. Mobility was seen as the key to transport and this was to be delivered by the motor car. Governments saw their role as catering for the increasing demand for car ownership by providing new roads. Clearly there has not been complete laissez-faire in transport policy because there is a complex web of planning decisions, road inquiries, and innumerable regulations. In that sense, there has been a fair amount of regulation of the process – with inquiries for new roads often leading to the abandonment of schemes – but this has modified a process which has been under way for forty years: the hegemony of the car.

Transport as Social Service

Public transport was seen to have elements of 'social service'. Hence the belief held by many people in government before 1979 that public transport was different and subsidies were inevitable – they are widely used in other European countries which have better transport systems than the UK. In the 1970s and 1980s it was local government which championed the idea of transport as a social service: in particular, the Greater London Council and South Yorkshire County Council. After the Conservative government had come to power in 1979 these two authorities found themselves at odds with the government over their transport policies.

In the Sheffield conurbation buses have greater importance than in some other conurbations because there is only a skeletal rail network (Hill, 1986, p. 100). South Yorkshire County Council had decided in 1974 that they would maintain bus fares at their 1974 level and this was held until 1984, a reduction of 30 per cent in real terms over this period (p. 99).

The council argued that many more people would use the buses as a result of the low fares and this would relieve traffic congestion in the Sheffield conurbation. Of course there were many social consequences: people living on the outskirts of the city found the journey to city centre shops much less prohibitive, and youngsters were able to travel to events on their own by bus rather than being reliant on their parents.

Research on the effect of the policy in Sheffield and South Yorkshire indicates that the biggest benefits were for those who were 'mobility deprived' either because of age or low income. Unemployed people appreciated the very low bus fares because they enabled them to keep up with activities which in other areas would have been impossible because of the high cost of fares – they could use the buses to travel to Sheffield city centre, to use the libraries and the shops. Elderly people appreciated the low fares for the same reasons and in addition they benefited from a travel pass which allowed free travel at off-peak times (Goodwin et al., 1983). In 1986 they were finally forced by the government to increase their fares and the resulting increase was 250 per cent. As a result between 1986 and 1991 bus passengers decreased by 30 per cent in the central area of Sheffield (*Independent*, 10 July 1991).

The GLC gained considerable publicity for its 'fares fair' policy in the early 1980s. This reduced fares markedly on buses and tubes: following a 25 per cent cut there was a freeze on increaes. Naturally it was very popular with public transport users but not with some of the Conservative-led outer London boroughs. On their behalf the London Borough of Bromley took the GLC to court and it was eventually ruled that it was illegal to subsidize fares in this way (Lansley, Goss and Wolmar, 1989, pp. 48–9).

Transport and Disadvantage

It is relatively straightforward to identify certain groups who suffer from a lack of mobility. But this is on the whole caused by their status, age, sex or handicap.

Children suffer from multiple mobility handicaps because of their age. In the age of the automobile their mobility position has actually deteriorated. Children's lives are circumscribed to an extent unimagined thirty years ago, because of fear. Children do not play on the streets to the extent that they used to. Their parents know the figures on road deaths and accidents (400 children are killed on our roads each year) and don't want their offspring to swell the numbers. Road accidents are the major cause of death and injury to children, accounting for a quarter of all deaths of school children and two thirds of all accidental deaths. One in fifteen children can expect to be injured in a road accident before their fifteenth birthday (Department of Transport, 1990). Another reason why children are not allowed the same freedom as children in the past is that parents are worried that their children will be abducted by sex offenders, and the ability of these people to commit their crimes has been aided by the motor car (Hillman, Adams and Whitelegg, 1990, p. 24). The children's world is thus more and more confined to the home and the garden (if they are lucky enough to have one). The home, which can be a haven of security for their parents from the stresses of work, can be a prison for a child. Children are treated in some ways like prisoners. Taken from one safe location – the parental home – in the family car, strapped in a child seat and then released under the watchful eye of the parent into another place of safety – school or a friend's house. Children of today are thus denied the street as personal play space.

Children's independent mobility has been greatly restricted by the tremendous increase in traffic. Thirty years ago it was quite common, even in built-up urban areas, for older children to use their bikes as a form of transport but nowadays many parents insist that these bikes just be used in the immediate vicinity of the child's home. Road conditions are dangerous for child cyclists. Another index of how children's independent mobility has been restricted by the rise in the use of motor cars is the number of young children who go to school on their own. A survey in 1971 showed that 80 per cent of seven and eight year olds went to school on their own but when the same survey was repeated at the same schools in 1990 it was found that the figure had dropped to 9 per cent. The main reason that parents gave for not allowing their children to travel to school on their own was the fear of traffic (Hillman, Adams and Whitelegg, 1991).

When children become teenagers their mobility problems can be felt quite acutely. The social life of teenagers can often be geographically widespread as many attend schools with large catchment areas, particularly in rural or semi-rural areas. If a teenager is living in a household without a car then opportunities to socialize or take part in after-school activities are limited unless friends' families can be persuaded to offer lifts. Understandably no one wants to be in a position where they are often asking for lifts. Of the alternatives, parents of teenagers are reluctant for them to walk home late at night or use public transport. Clearly these worries are greater for girls in a society where sexual attacks are increasing.

In a study of travel patterns of teenagers and young people in different areas of Glasgow, Bradley and Thompson found that there were marked differences between the numbers of journeys made by teenagers and young people in the middle-class areas they studied as opposed to the two working-class areas. In the middle-class district more than 90 per cent of households owned a car and more than half owned two or more; whereas for the two working-class districts one had a car ownership rate of 21 per cent while in the other it was only 10 per cent (Bradley and Thompson, 1981).

Teenagers in the middle-class district made nearly 50 per cent more trips than those in the working-class district. In the middle-class area it was a safe assumption that when they reached the age of seventeen teenagers could hope to gain a driving licence and use of a car whereas in the working-class districts this was unlikely. In these communities teenagers were much more dependent on the buses. We live in a society where fear of sexual attack is real for women. In the middle-class district 95 per cent of young women had a driving licence and independent use of a car and so they could feel they were relatively safe when travelling alone at night (1981).

At the other end of the life cycle the transport deprivation of elderly people is linked to increasing ill-health: their ability to get about declines; fewer of them at older ages have driving licences, fewer are able to use public transport and fewer are able to walk. Yet unlike children and young teenagers they are not barred from driving cars and the number of elderly people holding a driving licence continues to rise as the figures in table 4.3 show.

Table 4.3 Percentage of age group holding a car driving licence

Age Group	1965		1985		Increase 1985/1965	
	Male %	Fem. %	Male %	Fem. %	Male %	Fem. %
17–59	55	12	71	47	29	290
60–64	41	6	74	28	80	366
65+	19	2	57	14	200	600

Source: Department of Transport, The Older Road User, 1989, figure 3.

Nonetheless it is the case that 52 per cent of elderly people live in households without cars compared with 23 per cent of the general population (Potter and Hughes, 1990). Sometimes the cost of public transport is a serious disincentive to travel. Government has over the years responded to this problem in a number of ways. For many years local authorities have been enabled to run concessionary fares schemes for elderly and disabled people which give them reduced cost, usually half-price travel. The problem with concessionary fare schemes, as with all 'permissive' legislation in social policy is that some local authorities did not have any scheme. In Great Britain in 1978 out of the estimated 9.4 million persons over retirement age some 800,000 lived in areas which provided no concessions. In the 1970s the Labour government proposed that a national scheme be introduced to cover elderly and disabled people in these areas, allowing them to travel half-price on the buses whilst still permitting other local authorities to improve on this with a more generous local scheme, but this did not materialize (Department of Transport, 1979, 4.1). There are marked differences on travel concessions between one part of the country and another. In London, residents over pensionable age qualify for free travel on bus and underground services after 9 am on weekdays, all day weekends and on bank holidays. Other local authorities offer more limited concessions, usually half-price travel. Some local authorities offer no concessions at all for elderly and disabled people.

Many disabled people are losers in a society organized around the concept of mobility, as the very fact of their disability makes mobility difficult. We tend to think of transport in terms of journeys of a few miles or more using the roads but actually it can be the short journey, the visit to the local shops or doctor, which can be critical in people's lives and yet very difficult if they are disabled. Disabled people suffer the inconvenience of pavements not designed for wheechairs, and find so many buildings are closed to them because there is no wheelchair access. For longer journeys on public transport there are other problems. Few buses can take wheelchairs although there are a small number of specially adapted buses which are designed to do so. Trains can take wheelchairs although this often means having to travel in the guard's van, although new rolling stock with sliding doors on to the platform is being developed which makes carriages accessible to wheelchair users. The private car is the most commonly used form of transport for disabled people, probably because of the difficulties which disabled people experience in using public transport (Martin, White and Meltzer, 1989, p. xi). In a partial recognition of the fact that so many disabled people do not have an independent means of transport, the Mobility Allowance was introduced in the 1970s for people who are unable to walk to help them with the costs of fares and taxis. This has now been incorporated as the 'mobility component' of the Disability Living Allowance.

There is an extensive network of transport for elderly and disabled people provided outside of the public transport system. This is social services transport which can be the minibus used to take old people on a shopping trip, or the bus which takes disabled people to a club or a day centre. But should special social services transport be seen as the answer? Many disabled people argue that what they require is the adaptation of public transport for people with disabilities. The Department of Transport's advisory committee on transport for people with disabilities agrees. In a report trenchantly entitled *Mobility Policy for Britain's Entire Population* it argues that the transport system ought to be developed so that disabled people could use it rather than developing special services for them. It argues that disabled people's needs should be viewed alongside the transport needs of two other groups who cannot easily use public transport: the adults who are able-bodied but are encumbered with too much to carry and people who just do not have a bus service close enough to them to be able to use. In the United States since 1973 there has been a requirement that no government agency should discriminate against disabled people and this has led to sustained pressure for public transport to be adapted (Berkowitz, 1987). Clearly if an anti-discrimination measure for disabled people was introduced in the UK transport would be an early target for campaigners.

In addition to those groups of the population who have mobility problems there are also gender differences in access to transport. This can be viewed in two ways: 1) the major users of public transport are women, 2) a minority of women have a driving licence and research shows that they use the household car less frequently than men. Only 30 per cent of women hold a driving licence compared with 68 per cent for men (Pickup, 1988, p. 98). Research indicates that in a majority of households decisions as to car use were made on grounds of gender: 'The general pattern was for husbands to have the first choice of car use, usually for commuting, and for their wives to rely on using public transport or receiving lifts to meet their travel needs' (p. 103). But women who have the primary role in families for shopping and for escorting children home from school are more affected by the increasing trend towards out-of-town locations for shopping centres and greenfield sites for schools. Cuts in public transport affect women disproportionately as they are the majority of public transport users yet bus and train services are not responsive to their needs, particularly for shopping and child care (*Guardian*, 3 January 1991).

Road Accidents

There is a major health and social problem in this country which most of us prefer not to think about: road traffic accidents. Around 5,000 people die every year on our roads (Potter and Hughes, 1990, p. 9). If this order of deaths and serious injuries was being caused by a virus then the research effort devoted to finding a cure would be enormous. Yet there is little public outcry about these figures, and most people accept them as part of an inevitable consequence of our way of life. In addition to the often highly skilled treatment which road accident victims require, sometimes involving months of in-patient care, there are other costs to the economy – lost production, insurance costs and the cost of compensation claims in the legal system – which have been estimated at over £2 billion a year (*Guardian*, 7 June 1990). Road accidents represent a major drawback to living in urban areas. Whitelegg has shown that in 1982, in the ten member states of the EEC (excluding Spain and Portugal) 72.6 per cent of the accidents were in built-up areas, while in the UK 95 per cent of pedestrian accidents occurred in built-up areas and 95 per cent of child pedestrian accidents occurred within a quarter of a mile of the child's own home (Whitelegg, 1988, p. 90).

Government maintains that road deaths are declining in this country by citing the fact that in 1982 there were close on 6,000 road deaths a year while now the figure is nearer 5,000. But this figure needs to be examined by category of road user, and then we find that deaths among all the non-motorized travelling public have increased. Among children who have achieved some form of independence in their mobility, roughly from age ten upwards, there has been an increase in deaths and accidents. The death and serious injury rate among the ten to fourteen age group has almost doubled over the last thirty years: in 1958 it was 36 per 100,000 population and in 1988 it was 69 per 100,000 population (Department of Transport, 1989). Children are one of the most vulnerable groups but so too are elderly people: one in three of the pedestrians killed on our roads is over the age of seventy: see table 4.4.

The real tragedy behind these figures is that most of the accidents are due to human negligence and could have been prevented. As more and more traffic comes onto the roads the need for careful, courteous driving becomes paramount yet this is clearly not occurring. One of the major causes of accidents is excessive speed yet in the mid-1980s it was reported that 40 per cent of drivers exceed the

Table 4.4 Pedestrian accident fatality rates

Age group	Pedestrian fatality rate Per 100 million km	Pedestrian fatality rate Per 100,000 population	% of Population
0–4	4.6	1.6	
5–9	8.4	2.7	18.8
10–14	5.1	2.8	
15–19	3.7	2.3	7.9
20–59	4.5	1.7	52.5
60–64	8.7	3.3	
65–69	10.7	4.3	20.8
70–74	22.5	7.3	
75+	66.4	12.0	
All	7.9	3.1	100.0

Source: Mayer Hillman 'The neglect of walking in transport and planning policy' in Transport 2000, *Transport and the Pedestrian*, 1989.

speed limit and more than 50 per cent of drivers do so in residential areas (Caudrey, 1986).

There are many reasons why drivers flout the law in this way – one major reason is police inactivity. It may be that for many policemen the fact that so many drivers exceed the limits is a reason why they are not vigilant but then this becomes a reason why motorists choose to ignore speed limits. The chances of getting caught for speeding are estimated to be one in 7,600 (Whitelegg, 1988, p. 94). For other road users the fact of excessive speed, drivers travelling at 40 mph in built-up areas where the limit is 30 mph, constitutes a major hazard. In 1978 13 per cent of new car models were capable of doing more than 120 mph – by 1990 that figure had risen to 40 per cent. The proportion of cars that could accelerate to 60 mph in under ten seconds rose from 22 per cent in 1978 to more than 50 per cent in 1990 (Potter and Hughes, 1990, p. 7).

In a society where speed is used to sell cars and where speed is regarded as 'sexy', it is not surprising that the flouting of speed limits should occur. Motor manufacturers must bear a major responsibility for building cars which can travel far in excess of the speed limits on our roads. There are many people who believe that the motor industry should take a more responsible attitude and stop using speed as an inducement to drivers to buy their cars. Because within the EEC there has been a reduction in the total of road deaths and accidents, this fact has been used to avoid lowering speed limits. Yet, as we have seen, the total figure can mask what is happening to particular groups of the travelling population – the non-motorists.

Road deaths and casualties are the most conspicuous and dramatic consequence of traffic congestion and more than 20 million cars on the roads of the United Kingdom. But there are other, equally disturbing, health effects. Table 4.5 below summarizes what are thought to be the main hazards resulting from pollutants.

The operation of a largely car-based transport system has meant that there have been other consequences for the public health. Children's physical health has declined in the post-war period and a number of authorities attribute this to the fact that children get less physical exercise than in the past, because they are more likely to be driven to school rather than walk and they are far less likely to play in the streets because of the danger from traffic.

Air pollution is now recognized as an important environmental and health problem; motor vehicles are the single most important cause of air pollution. Although there has been no systematic study of the health risk that motor vehicles pose a recent report concluded:

Table 4.5 Health hazards of pollutants from motor vehicles

Pollutant	Health hazards
Carbon monoxide	Deprives body of oxygen by reacting with haemoglobin. Slows thought and reflexes. Causes drowsiness and headaches. Long term exposure may aggravate arteriosclerosis causing cardiovascular disease. May retard foetal development in pregnant women. A 'greenhouse gas'.
Nitrogen oxides	Irritate lung tissue increasing susceptibility to viral infection, bronchitis and pneumonia. Responsible for one third of the acidity of rainfall. 'Greenhouse gases'.
Hydrocarbons and airborne particulates	Heavy metals and polyaromatic hydrocarbons carried deep into lungs on fine particulates are potentially carcinogenic. Irritate respiratory system.
Ozone	Irritates eyes, nose, throat and lungs causing coughing, headaches and reducing resistance to respiratory infections. Aggravates asthma and bronchitis. Implicated in damage to trees from acid rain. 'A greenhouse gas'.
Carbon dioxide	No direct health effects, but it is the most important 'greenhouse gas' contributing to global warming.
Lead	Impairs mental development in children.
Benzene	Associated with cancer, leukaemia and impotence.

Source: Transport and Health Study Group, *Health on the Move*, 1991, table 5.

Especially at risk at present are the 50 per cent of the population who are particularly susceptible to adverse air quality i.e. children, the elderly, asthmatics, pregnant women and unborn children, and sufferers from cardiovascular or respiratory disease. (CTC, 1991, p. 2)

There is mounting evidence which suggests that safe levels for nitrogen dioxide and carbon monoxide levels are being exceeded on a regular basis in urban areas. In rural areas there is a problem with high levels of ozone which exacerbate respiratory conditions. Asthma is a growing problem with the number of sufferers growing at the rate of 5 per cent a year (CTC, 1991, p. 5). Some link this to the increase in traffic congestion and air pollution.

The unhealthiness of motor transport for drivers, their passengers and other road users seems clear. Other forms of transport – walking and cycling – are beneficial for the body, encouraging greater activity by the heart and improving the respiratory system. Studies show, for instance, that people who cycle regularly experience a heart attack rate lower than that for motorists and less than half that of the population in general (CTC, 1991, p. 17).

Mobility or Access?

The reduction of deaths and accidents on our roads would be a welcome and highly important outcome of the imposition of lower speed limits, or merely the enforcement of existing limits, but there are other considerations. A safer environment would also be a more pleasant environment with a reduction in traffic noise and because the streets were safer, would offer more opportunities to use them. The street used to be the focal point of city life, not just a means of getting from one location to another but a place where people met one another, goods were bought and sold by traders or at markets, where there were various forms of entertainment and, occasionally, where people would try to influence their fellow citizens by standing on a soap box to sell their political views. When the advance of suburbanization has made many facilities too far distant from non-car-using city dwellers, then there is a revival of interest in constructing a new environment for the city in which walking, cycling and public transport would be the dominant means of travelling. In order to achieve this the car dependency of the population will need to be reduced and this would be an objective of an environmental policy which prioritized the reduction of carbon emissions. The opinion surveys quoted earlier in this chapter show that the only way to stop people using their cars and encourage them to move to other forms of transport is to increase significantly the price of petrol. Cities need to become safer places and streets need to regain some of their lost sociability. In our society mobility is prized and praised. Yet in the 1990s the price of the pursuit of mobility is having to be paid in permanently congested town centres and increased pollution. The fact is that not so many people are as 'mobile' as is assumed, and many do not have the use of a car for personal transport. The inequalities of sex, age, disability and class are reproduced in our transport system. If the trend of transport policy continues to be informed by the concept of mobility then the position looks bleak for the one third of households who do not have access to a car, because the organization of our society will move towards more decentralization of shops, places of work and public facilities. Access is now regarded as a more useful concept in transport policy because it enables us to plan for the entire population. If we believe in access then not only are we committed to providing wheelchair entrances for buildings but also an expansion of public transport so that many more people can enjoy the leisure and work opportunities which today are often reserved for motorists.

Discussion Questions

1 How would our transport system differ if it were organized around the concept of accessibility?
2 Is the motor car at the root of Britain's transport problems?
3 How can social policy compensate for the transport disadvantages suffered by some people in our society?

Suggested Further Reading

There are a number of recent publications which look at the social impact of transport. John Roberts et al. (eds), *Travel Sickness: the need for a sustainable transport policy for Britain* (Lawrence and Wishart, 1992) is a wide-ranging and comprehensive collection of essays. On health see the Transport and Health Study Group report, *Health on the Move* (1991). For a positive and environmentally friendly alternative to the car see Mayer Hillman, *Cycling Towards Safety and Health* (Oxford University Press, 1992). Policy in the context of environmental concerns is explored in John Whitelegg, *Transport for a Sustainable Future*, (Belhaven Press, 1993).

References

Bagwell, P S (1984), *End of the Line? The Fate of British Railways under Thatcher*, London: Verso.

Berkowitz, E D (1987), *Disabled Policy: America's Programs for the Handicapped*, Cambridge: Cambridge University Press.

Bradley, M and Thompson, S (1981), *Getting There: a survey of teenagers and young women, using cars or living without them in Glasgow*, Scottish Consumer Council.

Buchanan, C (1964), *Traffic in Towns*, London: Penguin/HMSO.

Caudrey, A (1986), 'Fast living, fast death', *New Society*, 1 August.

Cyclists Touring Club (CTC) (1991), *Bikes not Fumes*, London.

Department of Transport (1979), *Concessionary Fares for Elderly, Blind and Disabled People*, Cmnd 7475, London: HMSO.

Department of Transport (1989), *Road Accidents Great Britain 1988*, London: HMSO.

Department of Transport (1989) *Roads to Prosperity*, Department of Transport (1990), *Children and Roads: a safer way*, London: HMSO.

Department of Transport (1991), *The Older Road User*, London: HMSO.

Disabled Person's Transport Advisory Committee (1990), *Mobility Policy for Britain's Entire Population*, London: HMSO.

Goodwin, P B et al. (1983), *Subsidised Public Transport and the Demand for Travel: the South Yorkshire Example*, Aldershot: Gower.

Goodwin, P B et al. (1991), *Transport: the new realism*, Transport Studies Unit, University of Oxford.

Hill, R (1986), 'Urban Transport: from technical process to social policy' in P Lawless and C Raban (eds), *The Contemporary British City*, London: Harper and Row.

Hillman, M and Whalley, A (1979), *Walking is Transport*, London: Policy Studies Institute.

Hillman, M, Adams, J and Whitelegg, J (1991), *One False Move: a study of children's independent mobility*, London: Policy Studies Institute.

Lansley, S, Goss, S, and Wolmar, C (1989), *Councils in Conflict: the rise and fall of the Municipal Left*, London: Macmillan.

Martin, J, White, A and Meltzer, H (1989), *Disabled Adults: services, transport and employment*, London: HMSO.

National Consumer Council (1987), *What's Wrong with Walking? A consumer review of the pedestrian environment*, London: HMSO.

Pickup, L (1988), 'Hard to get around: a study of women's travel mobility', in J Little et al. (eds), *Women in Cities*, London: Macmillan.

Potter, S and Hughes, P (1990), *Vital Travel Statistics*, Transport 2000.

Sherlock, H (1990), *Cities are Good for Us*, Transport 2000.

Stancliffe, A (1992), 'Voyage of destruction', *New Statesman and Society*, 3 January.

Sutton, J (1988), *Transport Coordination and Social Policy*, Aldershot: Avebury.

Transport 2000 (1990), Roads Report.

Transport and Health Study Group (1991), *Health on the Move*, Birmingham.

Whitelegg, J (1988), *Transport Policy in the EEC*, London: Routledge.

5

SHOPPING

In an industrial society shopping is an essential means of obtaining food and other basic necessities. But in the late twentieth century we have been persuaded to stop thinking of shopping as a chore which has to be done in order to get our food, buy our clothes, our household appliances. Instead many people now think of shopping as a 'fun activity', and indeed believe that shopping will provide them with an identity – whether it be through the acquisition of an item of clothing, or a particular record or tape. Shopping is now one of our most popular leisure activities according to a recent survey (Mintel, British Lifestyles Report, *Guardian*, 7 February 1990). Shopping is also big business. Retailing employs more than two million people (O'Brien and Harris, 1991, p. 50). This chapter looks at the expansion of shopping, particularly since 1945, focusing on changes in the location of retail developments and assessing their consequences for disadvantaged groups in our society.

Telecommunications are changing the nature of retail organization and the way we shop, and we consider the extent to which they will lead to better shopping provision. The retail expansion of the 1980s was fuelled by a tremendous increase in credit, both for the shops selling the goods, many of whom expanded beyond their capacities, and for the shoppers, some of whom found themselves saddled with insupportable debts. The emphasis given to shopping in our society has led many people to argue that we have become a 'consumer society'. Some critics see consumerism as an overpowering ideology which extinguishes moral values while others welcome consumerism for the opportunities it offers to celebrate and express identity and style. We review this debate and discuss whether the change in the nature of shopping reflects social change or promotes it.

The Rise of Shopping

When Napoleon described the British as a 'nation of shopkeepers' he was not referring to multiples, supermarkets or chain stores. Shopping in the nineteenth century was a very different affair. In large towns and in the cities shopping for food was done in open air markets. The markets would be selling produce taken direct from the surrounding countryside. It was in the mid-nineteenth century that the first covered municipal market was built in Liverpool (Davis, 1966). Then shopping differed greatly from region to region: in towns and cities some streets only catered for the middle-class shopper. The working class did have shops but 'they were few, meagrely stocked and struggling to counterbalance bad debts by high prices' (pp. 262–3). The Co-operative Societies emerged in the 1840s to provide low cost, unadulterated food for working-class people. This was a different form of shop in that the shoppers were encouraged to join the society and thereby receive part of the profits which were distributed to members as a 'dividend'. Throughout the nineteenth century the poor shopped in street markets. By the mid-nineteenth century shops catering exclusively for the middle classes opened – the department stores. These combined under one roof services normally provided by different shops: clothing, perfumeries, food, household goods, wools etc. They had a great appeal to women and the French writer Zola was to describe them as 'a temple to women, making a legion of shop assistants burn incense before her' (Urry, 1990, p. 152).

The chain store aimed at the mass market emerged in the late nineteenth and early twentieth centuries. Marks and Spencer made a reputation for selling good quality items at a reasonable price. The American company, Woolworth, opened their first store in the UK in 1909. Food retailing was also changing. Among the grocers, shops found in every town before the Second World War the High Street firms, Lipton and Sainsbury, were the largest.

Supermarkets

The supermarket arrived in Britain in the early 1950s when Tesco was the first chain to open shops where customers could pick up goods themselves and put them in a basket and then take them to the 'check-out'. Sainsbury followed suit and the new supermarkets began to kill off the corner shops which had been a feature of nearly every street in the towns and cities of Britain. Greater mobility was a major factor. The increasing availability of motor cars from the 1950s meant that people could now shop for food outside their neighbourhood more easily. Because supermarkets bought large quantities of goods they were able to undercut prices of small grocers. The spread of the refrigerator meant that more people could buy in bulk from the new supermarkets. A major retailing change had occurred. Since 1961 nearly three quarters of grocers have disappeared.

Supermarkets organized on the basis of self-selection of goods were an innovation in the High Street. But the next stage of retailing saw the weakening of the High Street, because from the 1970s retailers began to realize that it was becoming increasingly difficult to attract more shoppers to their stores in overcrowded city centres. Often supermarkets lacked their own car-parks and although many chains bought new inner-city sites made vacant by the widespread demolition and replanning of city centres this land in central locations was sold at a high price. The next development was the rise of the superstore – the very large store on the outskirts of a town or city – usually defined as having a floor space of at least 2,500 square metres together with ample car parking space. In the 1990s the new Tesco's stores have a minimum size of 10,670 square metres whereas in the 1970s it was 3,048 square metres. Because the profit margins are so low food retailing has been forced to be one of the most dynamic sectors, although it is argued that the move to out-of-town locations and the saving on manpower have not been reflected in lower prices and this accounts for the big rise in profits of the grocery retailers in recent years (TEST, 1989).

Shopping and the Urban Environment

If firms in other sectors have been less innovative this does not mean that they have not followed in the path of the food retailers. The move to out-of-town locations has also been effected by other High Street multiples. The 'High Street' has seen the loss of thousands of hardware stores in the last twenty years as the large Do It Yourself retailers squeeze them out of existence. The related store development of the 1970s was the hypermarket, which is usually a hybrid of grocery store and durable goods: for instance, there have been a number of joint hypermarket developments involving Sainsbury and British Home Stores. Smaller furniture shops have been likewise forced to close down because of the growth of large retailers who have increasingly based their business around the retail warehouse on the edge of the town, catering for the car-driving shopper. The trend is also seen in the electrical and 'white goods' chains which sell fridges, televisions and washing machines. Commonly two or three of these retailers will be found occupying the same 'retail park' (Montgomery, 1987).

The costs of these developments are first borne by those who live in the city centres, where the range of stores narrows as the supermarkets close and the main food outlet for those without transport then becomes the small (and expensive) grocer. There is also a loss of jobs for those people who live in or near the city centres where the job gains associated with the new retail developments are not as great as is often claimed. A study for Portsmouth City Council showed that of the 200 new jobs needed for a retail park only 50 were, in fact, new ones the rest being relocation of staff from other outlets (TEST, 1989). The visual appearance of the city centre changes as well. The large shops act as the focal point for a shopping centre, 'the anchor stores' and their closure, when they move to out-of-town locations, means a fall in trade for the smaller retailers who are left behind. When they too close, as many of them are forced to do, then the High Streets are in danger of becoming places where one finds only branches of banks, building societies and other nationally controlled organizations. Local business disappears from the High Street. The sites formerly occupied by Marks and Spencer or Sainsbury may remain unoccupied for months or years giving the shopping centre a downbeat look, a form of blight which makes the entire area a less attractive shopping district. Yet there is another kind of blight, that of graffiti and litter or the youngsters who hang around these centres particularly when they are closed and cause vandalism (Davies, 1987). Past planning policies have designated the centres of many of our cities as retail and office areas only, so that when these have closed the district is empty. This is a British phenomenon – in other countries people continue to live in the city centres so that they remain residential districts where everything does not close down at 5 each evening.

Women and Shopping

In a patriarchal society it is clear that most types of shopping are seen as women's work. As traditional sex roles change – although the change may only be at the margins – the identification of shopping with women is changing too. In the 1950s it would have been a rare occurrence to see men doing the weekly food shopping but no longer. In large part the identification of food shopping with women's role is the related fact that meal preparation is seen as the woman's task and it is seen as part of a woman's nurturing role. But there are obviously differences between kinds of shopping – shopping for clothes would be seen by most women as more pleasurable than shopping for food. A considerable amount of research has been conducted into the reasons why people shop and this shows that for women shopping fulfils several needs which were outlined by Rosemary Scott as personal and social reasons for shopping (Scott, 1976). First of all for many it is seen as part of their role as housewife; second, it is seen by some as a diversion from the house and from the children, although this is not true one suspects for mothers of pre-school children who have to be taken to the shops; third, shopping can be viewed by women as a form of self-gratification which combats boredom and loneliness; then again going to certain kinds of shops, particularly department stores, allows one to find out about new trends; it is a physical activity and a form of sensory stimulation for the individual woman. In addition to these individual psychological reasons for shopping there are obvious social motives as well. Shopping in itself is a social experience outside the home which can offer communication with others with similar interests. Clearly these are motivations which stem largely from the social role of the housewife and one could predict that the same reasons to shop would apply to men who worked at home caring for the children and running the household. As is commonly observed, in many households women now have to do the job of running the home and go out to paid employment as well. Retailing has changed to accommodate this fact, with sales of convenience food booming.

There are real problems for some women in shopping. There is often a lack of provision for women with children, and facilities for nappy changing or play areas could be increased. But a major problem given the continuing shift of food stores to out-of-town locations is the lack of access to motor cars by women. In 1980 31 per cent of women were qualified to drive as compared with 68 per cent of men (Grieco et al., 1989, p. 22). But the number of women who have access to a car is less than this percentage suggests, as their husbands may well use the car to get to work and thus it is unavailable for shopping during the day. Bus services are inadequate in many parts of the country and for women with small children buses are difficult

Table 5.1 Frequency of travel for each journey purpose by women

	5+ days a week	1–4 days a week	About once or twice a month	Less often	Never
Paid work	38%	10%	–	–	52%
Unpaid work/voluntary work	1%	8%	3%	2%	86%
Basic shopping	24%	64%	4%	1%	6%
Other shopping	1%	19%	45%	29%	7%
Escorting others	14%	8%	8%	4%	66%
Social/entertainment	7%	48%	24%	12%	9%
Other	1%	5%	1%	1%	92%

Source: M Grieco et al. (eds) (1989), Gender, Transport and Employment.

to negotiate with shopping and a pushchair. The London Travel Survey of 1985 showed that 88 per cent of women shopped for basic items at least once a week (see table 5.1).

The frequency of shopping trips is considerable, according to the London Travel Survey:

> A quarter of women go out shopping for basic (grocery) items at least five days a week and a further 64% go out at least once a week. Only 6% of women never go out shopping for basic items. Shopping for other items (e.g. clothes, furniture) is also important for women, with 20% of women going out at least once a week and nearly half of women travelling at least once a week or twice a month. 23% of all trips women make are for shopping compared to only 13% for men. (Focas in Grieco et al., 1989, p. 156)

The Shopping Needs of Elderly People

Shopping becomes more difficult with age. The UK General House-hold Survey (GHS) found that 16 per cent of people over 65 could not do shopping for themselves. Difficulties are acute for very elderly women, who are particularly likely to have difficulty walking down the road on their own, and the GHS reported that for women aged 80 to 84 one third could not shop on their own. For women aged 85 or more then it was found that two thirds could not shop on their own (OPCS, 1986). Likewise the GHS found that under a half of people in the oldest age-groups were likely to travel on public transport and were the most likely group among the elderly to need help if they did so. The GHS found that under a half of people aged 80 to 84 and only one third of those 85 or older used public transport (p. 182).

In Abrams's survey of the shopping needs of the elderly population he reported that:

> The incidence among elderly shoppers of ill health and health deficits that could affect their shopping behaviour is considerable: over 90% are short-sighted, over half suffered from arthritis/rheumatism, and almost half said they could not walk for half an hour without difficulty; and nearly half are less than 5′ 4″ in height – i.e. well below the height of many top shelves in the supermarkets they use. (Abrams, 1985, p. 8)

Modern stores are not designed with the elderly in mind and the crowding that takes place in some stores will deter many elderly people from shopping there, especially if they are frail. Elderly people interviewed for the Abrams study complained that they got very tired when shopping, had long waits for public transport and found the stores unpleasantly crowded. Even if a store bus is provided then the amount of carrying heavy bags that using such a service entails makes it prohibitive for many.

To shop on any scale you need to have access to transport, either public or private, and it is here that the difficulties of elderly people can be seen very clearly. Abrams found that less than a quarter of the survey (22%) had access to a car – either driven by themselves (12%) or by somebody else in the same household (10%). The survey also revealed that such access was much higher among the young elderly, that is those aged 65 to 74 (27%) than among the group aged 75 and over where it was 16% (Abrams, 1985). Of the elderly people in the UK over 60% do not have access to a car.

Those elderly people who travel to the shops either walk to the nearest store, which because of mobility problems would need to be within, say, half a mile, or go by bus. Buses present numerous actual and potential difficulties for elderly people in England. Since the general introduction of one-man operator buses (excluding London) elderly people who find it difficult to get on or off the bus have had more problems, for the helping hand of the conductor is no longer there. A common complaint is that the steps to buses are too high and elderly people often find it difficult to make their way along the bus carrying shopping. Only a certain amount of shopping can be carried by elderly people, even if they are fit and healthy, and once they have got off the bus they are then faced with the task of carrying the shopping back to their home.

It might be said that elderly people, because they were brought up in an era when the corner shop was widespread, must feel the loss of such stores nowadays more than the rest of the population. Certainly we can say that modern retailing is not geared to the needs of elderly consumers who wish to purchase small amounts. Supermarket chains make their profits from the shoppers who buy large quantities of goods – elderly people will shop with a basket, but it is the people who push the trolleys who make the profits for the supermarkets. Elderly people also suffer from the most obvious disadvantage: they are less prosperous than the general population. In the Abrams study 57 per cent were assessed as being poor, and this obviously limits their shopping choices (Abrams, 1985, p. 12).

Disadvantaged Shoppers

The shopping problems described here are part of the wider difficulties which result from the reorganization of retailing in the late twentieth century. It would appear that a process of social segregation is emerging in shopping where low income, carless consumers are losing their access to the big superstores which offer the best choice of goods. In the city centres a range of low cost stores are opening which cater for the needs of low income shoppers but only offer a restricted range of goods. In the past decade large numbers of smaller High Street supermarkets have closed. The decline in inner-city shopping is a serious issue for if it continues we could be witnessing the phenomenon of many American cities where the inner-city areas have experienced what is termed 'the doughnut effect': so-called because the central area loses its vitality with the movement away of shops and businesses. Already there is mounting concern about the health and physical condition of central shopping areas in the UK. The problems of litter, vandalism and vagrants, and a lack of amenities such as public telephones and toilets in many cities contribute to a general malaise. The job losses that come about from the move away from the city centre by retailers can thus be seen as the latest stage of the wider inner-city job losses which have occurred over the last thirty years as firms have relocated on the periphery of cities or in the more attractive location of small towns.

Access to low cost healthy food is important for all of us, especially for families with small children. Studies reveal nutritional deficiencies in the population which are concentrated in low income households. Households of this type eat more processed meat products, margarine, sugar and jam which are cheap energy sources but have high fat or sugar content (Cole-Hamilton and Lang, 1986, p. 44). Unsurprisingly foods are selected on the basis of cost. Low income households eat more potatoes, white bread and baked beans and less cheese, poultry, fish, frozen or fresh vegetables (p. 44). In a survey carried out in 1991, of 354 families with children under five in low income households, parents were asked if they had given their children certain foods regularly – some were those needed for a healthy diet and others were less healthy foodstuffs. As the authors comment: 'Fatty meat and meat products were eaten more often than lean meat and fish. Less than half the children and nearly two thirds of the parents did not eat fruit or green vegetables every day, and nearly three quarters of the families did not eat brown or wholewheat bread' (National Children's Home, 1991, p. 6). Among the constraints noted by the authors of the NCH report are the costs of getting to shops. In their study only 23% of families had access to a car. These costs have to be added to the cost of the weekly shopping basket and in their survey the NCH found that travel costs varied from zero to £5 a week (p. 8). In a recent survey Joffe remarks of the UK population: 'Deficiencies in vitamins and minerals and low intakes of fibre are commonplace. The most seriously affected groups are low income families, the elderly, people with disabilities, and increasing numbers of homeless people' (Joffe, 1991, p. 51).

New Technology

Information Technology has already made a considerable impact on the way in which we shop in this country. We do not need to use cash to shop any more as credit cards have become so widespread. Many major retailers now have Electronic Point of Sale (EPOS) equipment which enables them to identify the price from the bar code and thus do without having to price-label thousands of goods each week. In addition there are a number of homebanking and homeshopping services now available because of advances in Information Technology.

The development of EPOS has meant that stores can now speed up their ordering and distribution process because each store manager has the data at the end of each day, from the computer, on which product lines need to be replaced. EPOS also enables stores to conduct on-the-spot market research in that they can quickly see if a new line is selling well or not. It also increases the information available to the head office as the takings from each branch become available at the end of each day. The system now means that retailers can cut down the storage time between goods leaving the manufacturer and reaching the shop. It has been claimed by one leading food retailer that a store can order goods at 10 one night and the delivery will be made at 6 the next morning!

So there are considerable advantages and savings for retailers from EPOS, but we need to remember that there is a downside. Customers who have poor eyesight, overwhelmingly elderly people, now find it much more difficult to find out how much an individual item costs. Whereas pre-EPOS they would pick the tin of baked beans up so that they could read the price label, now they have to peer for the small price card on the shelf which is usually written in small type! One might also hazard a guess that shoppers generally are now less aware of the price of goods.

Another innovation produced by information technology is tele-shopping or computerized home shopping. This has been possible since the late 1970s since the introduction of videotext, an interactive computer-based information system. The best known and first viewdata service was British Telecom's Prestel which was launched in 1979. Large claims were made for Prestel, especially in the area of home shopping, but it has proved largely unattractive to the UK population and in 1991 there were only 90,000 subscribers, half of whom were business users, so its domestic base is tiny. The reason why it has proved so unattractive is that it requires the purchase of a home computer and a modem, a device which allows the information to be transmitted over the telephone. Nonetheless a number of mail order firms use Prestel and customers can order goods and pay for them in this way.

Teleshopping has an obvious relevance for housebound people and here it has been relatively successful. In 1981 Gateshead Social Services Department in association with Tesco started a teleshopping scheme for elderly and disabled people within the borough. This utilized a videotext system, similar to Prestel, which was available at selected day centres, sheltered housing units and libraries. Users could select items on the screen from a list of 3,000 and the order would be sent via the computer to the store and then delivered to the person's home. This was done without charge. A similar scheme was started in Bradford and Asda more recently provided a teleshopping service to several London social services departments.

The benefits of teleshopping for elderly and disabled people are amply attested to by the users. It is popular because it saves them the burden of carrying heavy shopping; it makes them more independent as they do not have to ask someone else to go down to the shops for them; it gives them more control as they do not have to rely on the judgement of someone else to select the items they require. But elderly people who are housebound may find the service less attractive in that they will find the trip to the shops a valuable outing in which there is the opportunity to meet other people, even if it is just a chat with the shop assistant.

Credit and Debt

The growth in popularity of shopping as a leisure pursuit was linked to the much easier availability of credit in the 1980s. Various restrictions on consumer borrowing were lifted and with the deregulation of the finance sector many more institutions became interested in entering the lucrative personal credit market. Overall, credit grew by around 18 per cent a year (National Consumer Council, 1990, 1.2.1).

Much of the retail expansion was funded by credit. It is reckoned that around a third of all consumer goods are now bought on credit (Berthoud, 1989, 2.2). This was partly through the growing popularity of bank credit cards but in addition, the big stores themselves began to introduce their own credit cards in the belief that where a person has a credit card then they will tend to buy more than if they had to pay by cash (Ford, 1988, p. 826). In 1988 the Burton Group had 25 per cent of the retail credit market while Marks and Spencer's own card had a 14 per cent share although it had only been launched four years earlier (NCC, 1.2.4). The Do It Yourself retailers have also sponsored an increase in credit.

Traditionally home shopping or mail order had been the way to obtain credit while shopping for goods and was mainly of appeal to women. It was a way for working-class families to finance purchases of costly items such as clothing or household goods, with an agent selling to friends and family on a commission basis. The easier availability of credit through credit cards meant that the demand for this agency catalogue business sharply declined. Instead mail order firms moved into selling to individuals and households and the 1980s saw the mail order firms move upmarket: this was typified by the launch of the Next Directory in 1988, a lavish production, aimed at style conscious 'yuppies'.

The number of bank credit cards increased enormously in the 1980s: in 1978 there were 8 million but by 1988, 25 million (NCC, p. 4). General bank lending, aside from their credit cards, increased during the 1980s so that in 1988 65 per cent of outstanding credit, not for

Figure 5.1 Sources of consumer credit, 1990

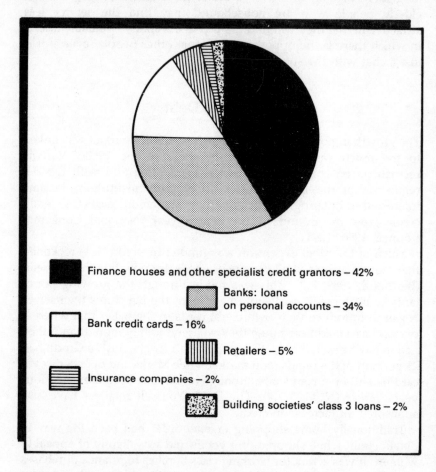

Source: R. Berthoud and E. Kempson, *Credit and Debt: the PSI Report.*

mortgages, was lending by the banks (p. 8). With financial deregulation building societies too entered the consumer credit market and there has been a proliferation of credit cards linked to building society accounts.

The relative share of the various financial institutions in 1990 is shown in figure 5.1.

Our attitude to credit seems to have changed. In the late 1970s when the National Consumer Council commissioned a survey of attitudes to credit among the general population, 20 per cent thought that it was a convenient way to buy things but by 1987 when the Office of Fair Trading investigated consumer attitudes 52 per cent selected convenience as the most important factor for using credit (NCC, p. 24). Clearly the tremendous rise in the number of credit cards in circulation must have changed attitudes. The NCC in their latest report came to the conclusion that there were major distinctions in the use of credit by social groups. Those in the higher income groups view credit as a convenient way to buy goods while people on low incomes think of credit as a way of obtaining goods that they could not otherwise afford. It is with this group that credit can turn into debt.

The definition of credit and debt and the distinction between the two is a difficult area. Although we can say that credit is desirable spending while debt is used to refer to amounts of money that people find difficult to repay, the fact remains that the money outstanding on a credit card is still a debt owed to the credit card company by the consumer. We are not encouraged to think of it in this way, however, for obvious reasons: the number of Access and Visa cards in circulation would be much smaller if they were known as 'debt cards'.

A number of surveys indicate that, compared to the population as a whole, there are more families in debt with three or more children (NCC, 3.2.1). It seems that there are stages in the life of a family when debt is more likely to be incurred. One is when the children are born as it usually brings dependency on a single income: at the turn of the century Seebohm Rowntree showed the relationship between the birth of children and a family's likelihood of falling into poverty, and it seems that the same can be said of debt ninety years later. Here is an extract from a case study of a lady who received help from a money advice centre. An unplanned baby precipitated debt problems for herself and her partner:

> We had money problems before the baby was born but somehow they didn't seem so bad. We just about kept even. Then after I got pregnant, which was somewhat unexpected, things just went from bad to worse. We had both been working and we were just having a job meeting the bills and at the same time as paying the debts off were having to build a room on our mobile home – to make room for the baby. Then things got really difficult. We had to apply for a loan to build the extension, and then just buying the usual baby things, and then everything just got on top of us. (Hartopp, 1987, p. 48)

Unemployment, particularly long-term unemployment, is a period when people are more likely to use credit in order to manage. A survey of social security claimants in 1982 showed that some 40 per cent of households had some form of credit (Berthoud, 1989, pp. 19–20). There was considerable variation in credit usage between household types, with elderly people having the least amount of credit and families with children the most. This bears out the findings of other studies which show that there is a very low use of credit among elderly people. As Berthoud points out there are explanations for this: firstly, elderly people were brought up in a time when saving and thrift were cardinal virtues and banks had to be persuaded to give you a loan rather than as now when they are constantly trying to 'sell' you one; the second explanation is that elderly people are at a stage in their life when they have much less need of credit as their major life purchases – car, house etc. – have been achieved and children have left home.

Credit was readily available in the mid-1980s and many people, as we have seen, took advantage of it. With the high interest rates of the late 1980s many people found that they could not meet their outgoings as the cost of borrowing had increased significantly. Unfortunately the response of some people was to accept the offers of new loans which would, supposedly, help them to keep their homes, but because they often involved the remortgage of their home often ended in the loss of their home and county court orders. It is people who are in this position who often have recourse to Money Advice Centres.

The reform of the social security system in the mid-1980s meant that a new source of credit became available for poor people. The Social Fund was opened in 1988 and replaced the previous system of discretionary grants to social security claimants. Under the Social Fund most payments are made in the form of budget loans which have to be paid back over a certain period of time with the money being deducted from the claimant's benefit each week. No interest is charged. The Social Fund has not been popular with social security claimants for a number of reasons: it is inflexible, the weekly income from benefits is reduced and people feel a sense of stigma in receiving the loans (Ford, 1991, p. 46).

Credit unions provide a cheap source of finance for low income families and individuals. Loans to members are generated from the savings made by the members. The interest rate charged to loan recipients is lower than that of a bank or building society. Credit unions are of most value to poor people who have difficulty finding a loan from the conventional sources – finance houses, banks, building societies and so forth. They are a fairly recent creation in Great Britain where they have only existed since the Credit Union Act of 1979 made them possible. In Northern Ireland they have been in existence much longer and are much more popular, although they are to be found almost exclusively in Catholic areas as the Roman Catholic church has long been a champion of credit unions.

But there are other shopping 'casualties'. The emphasis given by advertising and the media to shopping has meant that some people when depressed will go on a shopping spree in order to cheer themselves up. These 'shopaholics' are, literally, addicted to shopping. For them shopping has become a way of life, a pervasive form of fantasy. There are those who would maintain that this is but an extreme version of the consumerist ideology which dominates our society.

Privatized Shoppers

In the post-1945 world the dominant change was the creation of a consumer society in which household appliances have become a staple and commonplace part of most people's lives: see table 5.2.

The home has become the centre of many people's lives and entertainment and leisure now revolve around it. The introduction of the television, video and other home entertainment systems soon to be launched mean that this is an irreversible shift towards the private. The home is regarded as a haven and a place of security by both men and women (Saunders, 1990, pp. 304–10). People spend much more time in their homes than they did previously – the traditional working-class male pattern of going to the pub while the wife stayed at home has declined. Pub visits are now more likely to be made as a couple. The opportunity for retailers to sell more products has greatly increased with the post-war rise in real disposable incomes. Accompanying this focus on the home has come a more recent stress on 'lifestyle'. The origins of this term are difficult to fathom: it seems to come out of the world of Sunday colour magazines where it denotes 'essential' information about cooking, wine, clothes and the like. To that extent it can be said to be a creation of advertising, for what these articles are actually interesting readers in is a range of products. At a deeper level it might be said that lifestyle is a new phenomenon in that it reflects the belief that individuals can make a statement about their view of the world and their own position in it through the clothes they wear, the car they drive, the food they eat. As older certainties of religion and political commitment waned in the post-

Table 5.2 Consumer durables by economic activity status and socio-economic group of head of household

Percentages of households with:	Socio-economic group of head of household									Economically inactive heads
	Economically active heads									
	Professional	Employers and managers	Intermediate non-manual	Junior non-manual	Skilled manual and own account non-professional	Semi-skilled manual and personal service	Unskilled manual	Total		
television										
colour	96	96	91	94	95	89	90	94		87
black & white only	3	2	6	5	4	9	8	4		10
video	67	76	66	63	74	65	60	71		25
deep freezer/ fridge freezer	88	91	85	84	87	79	75	86		61
washing machine	93	95	89	89	92	87	83	91		72
tumble drier	60	62	47	43	52	43	36	52		25
dishwasher	32	27	12	10	8	2	1	14		4
microwave oven	51	60	49	51	51	41	32	51		21
telephone	98	97	94	90	86	73	63	88		80
home computer	44	33	24	22	24	18	14	26		4
Base = 100%	473	1485	708	491	2059	785	224	6225		3840

Source: General Household Survey.

war period the way was open for a new emphasis in society on the self. The touchstone for many people has become the criterion of self-fulfilment, or self-realization, and with this new standard for judgement on life advertisers can then appeal to people with claims that a particular product would enhance their identity. This offers consumer capitalism immense opportunities to design products which appeal to an individual's aspiration for a certain lifestyle. Indeed, we have already slipped into the language of marketing where 'aspirations' are studied and 'lifestyles' promoted. The market niche is increasingly constructed in terms of appealing to an identity: whether that be to sell mountain bikes, personal organizers, fantasy comics or any of the other means by which individuals assert their identity in the late twentieth century.

Perhaps the originator of lifestyle shopping in Britain was the Habitat store group who, from the 1960s, made contemporary furniture designs available to a much wider market through self-assembly furniture. Once the young couple had assembled their first home with the help of Habitat they could think of starting a family, and here Mothercare came to their assistance with shops which stocked everything a baby or a pregnant mother might need – from nursing bras to high chairs. Both these stores produced catalogues which meant goods could be ordered by phone or post. This was lifestyle shopping, as the customers were expected to identify with the models displayed in the catalogues. But it was the 1980s which saw the major advance in the concept of lifestyle. Here it was a clothes firm, Next, appealing to a 'market segment' in their thirties who were affluent and concerned to wear fashionable clothes. Next was a lifestyle concept. Its stores were designed as clothing stores had never been before. 'Lifestyle' became a marketing tool in the 1980s. The popular expression of this was the identification of different status groups within the population: *dinkies*, who were dual income no kids; *yuppies*, young, upwardly mobile professionals; *Sloane Rangers*, members of the upper middle class with traditional values. Market research firms began to target people in terms of their 'lifestyle', and classify consumers accordingly:

The Status Seeker	. . . a group which is very much concerned with the prestige of the brands purchased.
The Swinger	. . . a group which tries to be modern and up to date in all of its activities. Brand choices reflect this orientation.
The Conservative	. . . a group which prefers to stick to large successful companies and popular brands.

The Rational Man	. . . a group which looks for benefits such as economy, value, durability, etc.
The Inner-Directed Man	. . . a group which is especially concerned with self-concept. Members consider themselves to have a sense of humour, to be independent and/or honest.
The Hedonist	. . . a group which is concerned primarily with sensory benefits. (O'Brien and Harris, 1991, p. 121)

The incorporation of Information Technology into the process of retailing has meant that retailers can now potentially access a great deal of data about shoppers. Credit cards are a precise way of mapping not just what consumers buy and when but also where. Market research has to be thorough for retailers cannot afford to site a store in the wrong location. The location of new large hypermarkets by the major supermarket chains is only done after a great deal of consumer information for different areas has been sifted and analysed. This will include household expenditure on product types, the purchasing power of the catchment area, the nature of the competition and the forms of transport available (O'Brien and Harris, 1991).

It is important that consumers have information at their disposal to assess the quality of goods and services. In this respect the laws affecting purchase of goods have improved in the last twenty-five years. The traditional advice to shoppers, 'caveat emptor' (buyer beware), put the onus on the consumer to check out goods before purchase. Now under the Sale of Goods (Implied Terms) Act there is the stipulation that goods should meet the claims made for them by retailer and manufacturer and if they do not they can be returned and money refunded. Some local authorities provide Consumer Advice Centres where dissatisfied members of the public can enquire about their legal rights in relation to goods and services. In all areas Trading Standards Officers are able to advise and assist members of the public.

In the sphere of consumer information one of the most important advances was the formation of the Consumers Association in 1957, best known through its publication *Which?* Month by month this publication has published research on products which have been tested in its laboratories. The organization is entirely dependent on membership for its income and accepts no advertisements in *Which?* magazine. In this way it has managed to maintain its identity as a completely impartial source of information.

Which? started life when commercial television was opening in many parts of the UK. The way in which advertisers could now gain access to millions of people in their own homes was obviously a major opportunity for them. The extent to which advertising is a necessary means of informing consumers about the products on offer to them, or moves beyond this and becomes a way of over-influencing the population towards regarding certain attitudes as acceptable is obviously open to debate. As Neil Postman and others have observed the way in which commercials operate nowadays is not to provide information but rather images which are meant to influence the viewer (1987). There are countless examples: cars are advertised in exotic surroundings where there is no other traffic on the road and images of romantic love often pervade car adverts, while adverts for soft drinks suggest sociability and sport. In a way this is what lifestyle is about – for it offers consumers a package of attitudes with the products on offer. Perhaps it is no coincidence that lifesyle retailing has come into its own after television has been the dominant source of information and news for people in this country for more than thirty years. Although not all advertisers and manufacturers are interested in charting the aspirations of the in-work population: it is argued that there will be a considerable market for videos and escapist literature among the 11 million people who were estimated to be living at below 60 per cent of the national average wage (*Sunday Correspondent*, 4 February 1990).

There is a sense in which the term consumer society is an accurate one. There are many activities of social life which are now dependent to a greater or lesser extent on the revenue supplied by sponsors or advertisers; sport is one of the most obvious but sponsorship has entered into theatre and the arts generally. The media of communication in our society now carry more advertising than ever before and the health of our newspapers depends upon their ability to attract advertising. And yet advertising and marketing cannot take people beyond a certain point unless they are appealing to a need or want which is present in the audience's lives, even if this is unconscious. The American author Stuart Ewen has argued that 'style' has a number of roles. It is important in the definition of self:

As one enters or falls into encounters with other people – intimates and strangers alike – style is a way of stating who one is: politically, sexually, in terms of status and class. Style is a device of conformity or opposition . . . To 'have a lot of style' is an accolade of remarkable personhood. (Ewen in Tomlinson, 1990, p. 43)

There are many arguments about the extent to which we are living in a consumer society, i.e. a society where the dominant values are about the acquisition of material wealth. In the mid-1950s the writer J B Priestley coined the phrase 'admass' to refer to a society where an entire economic and social system was dominated by the need to consume material goods, while later in the 1950s consumer society was defined by the American economist J K Galbraith as a society where people are evaluated by the products which they own and the value system is organized around the promotion of consumption (Galbraith, 1958). Jeremy Seabrook has castigated consumer societies for extinguishing people's visions of alternatives by the ceaseless search for self-gratification. He points out how recent a phenomenon consumerism is – it really only dates from 1945. In the view of Seabrook and others consumerism as a way of life is harmful – people undoubtedly enjoy more physical comforts and ease than their ancestors, but constant 'new' goods actually promote dissatisfaction with what they already have and they become less willing to trust themselves to do things, becoming dependent on goods. Consumerism has attained the status of a religion – the more influential because it is not acknowledged as such but is all-pervasive. For Jeremy Seabrook the recent past has been the highpoint of this materialist creed when the market has become a dominant metaphor in our society and individuals have been encouraged increasingly to think of themselves as consumers (Seabrook, 1990).

Seabrook is but the latest and the most popular of a line of writers from the Left who have castigated consumer capitalism for its harmful effects on the working class. For a long time, particularly after the 1951, 1955 and 1959 election defeats for Labour, consumerism was blamed for the loss of interest in socialist ideas. The Conservatives were thought to have successfully harnessed consumer durables, home and car ownership to their aid so that as working-class families became more affluent they lost interest in voting Labour. These arguments about the political consequences of consumerism were to reappear in the 1980s, this time with sections of the Left seeing it in a much more positive light, although again it was felt that the three Conservative election victories of 1979, 1983 and 1987 owed something to the evident materialism that characterized the 1980s – the 'loadsamoney' culture that permitted people to boast about their wealth when previously this had been thought of as 'un-British'. But this time round instead of an outright rejection of consumerism some writers argued that there needed to be an understanding of *why* consumerism was so appealing. What was it that made shopping so desirable? This view came from sections of the Women's movement and the Left. In opposition to the view that consumers are duped by the wiles of the advertising agency smartasses with their manipulation techniques honed by the latest research in pop psychology and marketing, these writers argue that the media are viewed in a critical light by consumers – if a product is bad it won't sell, never mind how many millions are spent on promoting it. The Women's movement, which in its early days saw the media as the enemy with its constant tendency to use attractive young women to sell products and to depict women as contented homebodies never happier than when making a meal or trying out a new washing powder, now sees the activity of consumption as a potential source of identity for women and a source of power as well as subordination. Mica Nava has pointed out that advertising does not manipulate people in any straightforward manner: the messages of the advertiser are beamed into a multiplicity of contexts and are then reflected upon by the public. To put it crudely, advertising is not brainwashing. Nava argues that consumerism has given women a new source of power and identity as they make many of the consumer decisions in a household (1992). Other critiques of the work of Seabrook condemn what they see as his puritanical reaction to the pleasures afforded by consumer capitalism: 'Consumer culture can be exciting, novel, convenient and fun; it can be energizing rather than enervating' (Tomlinson, 1990, p. 17). But these critics of Seabrook have to take into account the question of sustainability. If consumerism, through the medium of advertising, promotes dissatisfaction and the buying of new goods then does it have a place in a society which is trying to conserve natural resources? Or to put it another way, can the resources of the planet sustain the consumption patterns of the rich world?

To a limited extent there has been a recognition of the global issues concerned with our system of production and consumption through the phenomenon of 'green consumerism'. The Body Shop was an early expression of a green consumer consciousness in the UK. In the late 1980s this green consumerism spread from cosmetics to a wide range of goods reflected in the pages of the best-selling *Green Consumer Guide* (Elkington and Hailes, 1989). Consumers have over the years made their political views known through boycotts – notably through the world-wide campaign against South African goods – and this was extended with the promotion of 'green' products in the late 1980s which were supposedly more environmentally friendly – washing powder, washing-up liquid and the like.

The extent to which 'green consumerism' represents a coherent political statement is doubtful. It can be viewed as an option just for people in the rich world while others in the poor world have to make do with inferior products. The option of 'green consumerism' has to be seen within a society in which economic forces can promote unecological practices. Nappies are a good example. Every year in the UK 3.5 billion disposable nappies are used which take the wood from 3 million trees (Button, 1989, p. 124). But the alternative is available of terry nappies which can be used time and time again, do not consume valuable timber resources and, unlike disposables, do not cause a rubbish problem as each disposable nappy's contents can carry a range of bacteria and viruses. Green consumerism is seen as a useful step forward in raising consciousness, but nonetheless a first step (see Jacobs, 1991, pp. 41–4). It is all based on the market system: so people alive today can afford lots of money to pay for petrol-guzzling cars and as a result less oil is left over for future generations. Ted Trainer has written in his book entitled *Abandon Affluence!*: 'How affluent would we be, how much coke and wine we could have, how many holidays in the snow . . . if each of us were not getting over 2,000 litres of oil every year when the average Ethiopian must make do with 12 litres?' (1986).

Shopping and Social Policy

Shopping is changing fast in our society: Information Technology, the ceaseless search for higher profits by retailers, the changing patterns of work and leisure, the impact of the growing use of the motor car have all ensured this. Yet as we have seen the pace and direction of this change is seldom informed by discussion and debate about the possible options for the future. This is not new. We can imagine that very few people in the 1950s would have welcomed the demise of the corner shop. Yet it happened just as now inner-city supermarkets are closing each week to be replaced by out-of-town superstores. Still there is no inevitability about this process. In continental Europe, France and West Germany in particular, the same migration from town centre to greenfield site occurred and in both countries the government intervened with a set of regulations which effectively stopped this movement. Because food retailers and other large stores are so important for the kind of life that we lead, their goal of higher profit needs to be tempered with a concern for the needs and aspirations of people. The food that we eat is important for our nutrition and health. Food policy in particular can no longer be fenced off from the health and social policies of our society. But neither should other aspects of retailing be seen as just part of the market for they too have impacts on our social and public policies.

Discussion Questions

1 Why has shopping become such a popular leisure activity?
2 Should policy-makers try to reverse the trend towards out-of-town shopping centres? How could this be done?
3 How can the state best safeguard the interests of low income consumers?

Suggested Further Reading

For an exploration of many of the themes covered in this chapter see Larry O'Brien and Frank Harris, *Retailing: Shopping, Space, Society* (David Fulton, London, 1991). For a vivid account of how retailing changed in the 1980s see Carl Gardner and Julie Sheppard, *Consuming Passions* (Unwin Hyman, London, 1989). On credit and debt see Janet Ford, *Consuming Credit: debt and poverty in the UK* (Child Poverty Action Group, London, 1991).

References

Abrams, M (1985), *A Survey of the Elderly Shopper*, London: Age Concern.
Berthoud, R (1989), *Credit, Debt and Poverty*, Social Security Advisory Committee, London: HMSO.
Button, J (1989), *How To Be Green*, London: Century.
Cole-Hamilton, I and Lang, T (1986), *Tightening Belts: a report on the impact of poverty on food*, 2nd edn, London: London Food Commission.
Davies, R L (1987), *Help for the High Street*, London: Tesco.
Davis, D (1966), *A History of Shopping*, London: Routledge, Kegan Paul.
Elkington, J and Hailes, J (1988), *The Green Consumer Guide*, London: Gollancz.
Ford, J (1988), *The Indebted Society: credit and debt in the 1980s*, London: Routledge.
Ford, J (1991), *Consuming Credit: debt and poverty in the UK*, London: Child Poverty Action Group.
Galbraith, J K (1958), *The Affluent Society*, London: Penguin.
Grieco, M et al. (1989), *Gender, Transport and Employment: the impact of travel constraints*, Aldershot: Avebury.

Hartopp, A (ed.) (1987), *Families in Debt*, Cambridge: Jubilee Centre Publications.

Jacobs, M (1991), *The Green Economy*, London: Pluto Press.

Joffe, M (1991), 'Food as a social policy issue', in N Manning (ed.), *Social Policy Review 1990–1*, Harlow: Longman.

Montgomery, J R (1987), *Trade Winds: the changing face of retailing and retail employment in the South East – an alternative strategy*, The Seeds Association.

National Children's Home (1991), *Poverty and Nutrition Survey*, London.

National Consumer Council (1990), *Credit and Debt; the Consumer Interest*, London: HMSO.

Nava, M (1992), *Changing Cultures: feminism, youth and consumerism*, London: Sage.

O'Brien, L and Harris, F (1991), *Retailing: shopping, space, society*, London: David Fulton.

OPCS (1986), *General Household Survey*, London: HMSO.

Postman, N (1987), *Amusing Ourselves to Death*, London: Methuen.

Saunders, P (1990), *A Nation of Home Owners*, London: Macmillan.

Scott, R (1976), *The Female Consumer*, London: Associated Business Programmes.

Seabrook, J (1990), *The Myth of the Market*, Bideford: Green Books.

Tomlinson, A (ed.) (1990), *Consumption, Identity and Style*, London: Routledge.

Trainer, T (1986), *Abandon Affluence!*, London: Zed Books.

Transport and Environmental Studies (TEST) (1989), *Trouble in Store: retail location policy in Britain and Germany*, London.

Urry, J (1990), *The Tourist Gaze*, London: Sage.

6

WORKING

Work is central to the lives of people in advanced industrial societies in the late twentieth century as it supplies the wherewithal for the business of daily living. For the great majority of the population this is the way to obtain money. In earlier times, income could be obtained through the domestic economy, by the process of selling articles made at home or by the produce that one could grow, but for most people this is no longer an option. However, work is not the only way that individuals can obtain money in our society: the social security system also provides an income and there is a direct interrelationship between work and this system. As well as an income, work is also a source of social identity: it defines the way in which many people see themselves and can become part of their personality. But we should not regard paid work as being the only kind of work. Most of the work that is done every day is unpaid: the work of running a home, preparing meals, caring for children and other dependants. When it is costed the sums are considerable: an insurance company calculated that housewives on average work seventy hours a week, and taking all their tasks into account and paying them the going rate for the various component parts of their role – nanny, cook, cleaner, driver etc. – they would be paid £18,000 a year (*Independent*, 3 February 1993). This chapter examines some of the dimensions of work in our society – the return of long term unemployment, the feminization of the work force and the position of older workers – in order to assess the place of work, both paid and unpaid, in social life.

Work has been an intrinsic part of the state's income maintenance system since the creation of the Poor Law in 1601. In that statute provision was made for the building of workhouses where the poor could receive relief in exchange for work performed. It was not until the Victorian era that most of these workhouses were built and they then formed a central feature of a 'New' Poor Law whose rationale was to persuade poor people to stay in low paid employment by making the alternative, 'going to the house', as stigmatizing as possible. For the early Victorians who administered the Poor Law work was the test of character. Unemployment was seen to result from idleness and the function of the Poor Law system was to reinforce the work ethic for the poor. For most of the nineteenth century the dominant belief in society was that to be out of work was to a large extent the fault of the person concerned: it was only at the end of the century that unemployment was acknowledged as a social problem. Problems arose at the end of the nineteenth century as most unemployed men did not accept that if they were out of work then they should have to enter the workhouse. The granting of the vote to the working class meant that for the first time they had to be listened to in this respect and as a result, and in a very faltering fashion, we saw the beginning of Social Policy institutions outside the Poor Law.

In the early twentieth century the Labour Party argued for a 'right to work', and those members of the Liberal Party who were concerned with social policy realized that if the working-class were to take a full part in the society, as was urged on them by Liberal Party theorists, then they had to be enabled to have a say in society. This meant they would need work and if they were without it they would require some basic form of subsistence relief to ensure that they did not become totally drained of resources, both material and physical. The National Insurance Act of 1911 was one result of these debates. It enshrined the principle of insurance in the payment of unemployment benefits which between the wars was extended to the great majority of male workers. However, as the mass unemployment of the inter-war period demonstrated, this was of little use if the economy was not producing sufficient jobs. William Beveridge, who in his famous 1942 Report laid down the basis of the social security system for post-war Britain, made it plain that a commitment to full employment by post-war governments would be the bed-rock for his scheme. In 1944 the coalition wartime government published its White Paper on Employment Policy which pledged post-war governments to the pursuance of full employment as a central policy objective. This formed one of the cornerstones of the 'post-war consensus', the commitment of both Conservative and Labour parties to the mixed economy and the 'welfare state'.

The election of Mrs Thatcher to the leadership of the Conservative Party in 1975 was to lead to the end of this consensus. Apart from this, the policy of full employment was looking increasingly difficult to sustain in the mid-1970s with unemployment figures at over one million. The Thatcherites attacked the post-war consensus for contributing to the decline of Britain and did not view the maintenance of full employment as a central policy objective. In fact, Conservative governments since 1979 have seen their role as being to free the labour market so that various restrictions and regulations are removed. Wages councils lost their ability to determine the pay of those under twenty-one as the government felt that this was making labour costs too high, and they have now been abolished. In addition, the government, arguing for a change in the British approach to employment, has stressed the need for what it calls an 'enterprise culture': 'a wide range of institutions and activities must be remodelled along the lines of the commercial enterprise', while the population is encouraged to adopt the values of initiative and hard work which are said to constitute this culture (Keat and Abercrombie, 1991; Heelas and Morris, 1992). Given the high numbers of those without work the government has had to invest significant sums both in social security payments and in employment schemes, particularly those aimed at young adults.

The Importance of Work

Work is a highly contested area in our society. The discussion so far has been about one sort of work, paid employment, but work refers to doing something and inevitably has a great range of usages: voluntary work, household work, domestic work, caring work, child care. Along with the return of mass unemployment has come a concentration on work as a major form of identity. This was seen most clearly in the 1980s phenomenon of the 'Yuppies' who revelled in the amount of work that they did and the very high standard of living that they were able to enjoy as a result. The pre-eminent 1980s Yuppy artefact was the personal organizer which enabled them to create an impression of busyness and constant activity. There was something awfully ironic in the fact that while mass unemployment had returned to haunt the working class, sections of the middle class were glorying in the amount of work they did. The Yuppies had appropriated the Protestant work ethic but, unlike the Quakers and Methodists of old, had discarded the injunction to defer gratification. The Yuppy work ethic enjoined that if they worked long hours they should receive the reward no later than the end of the month in the shape of a big salary.

It would be mistaken to think that the recession of the early 1990s had put paid to this way of viewing work or that it was only ever confined to a group of 'young, upwardly mobile professionals' or 'dual income no kids households' ('dinkies'). Clearly there are myriad influences here which make work a central part of people's identity in a way never previously seen. Other ways of viewing oneself – of creating an identity – have declined. In an increasingly privatized world the messages of the culture seem to suggest that people should be concerned about the self: consumerism encourages a preoccupation with style of life never previously encountered. Nowadays it is all too common for middle-class women who have given birth to a child to be asked 'When are you going back to work?' or 'Are you working?' There seem to be two assumptions operating here: a woman should want to leave her child and go into paid employment, and child care and looking after a house are not work! This is part of a trend which sees domestic work as menial and child care as not real 'work'. For many women who do not have the support of other female members of the family to do the housework and child care then it means employing someone else, almost always a woman, usually on low rates of pay to be a domestic or a nanny to look after the children. There has been a considerable increase in the number of these low wage jobs.

Because of the small number of nursery places in Britain childminding is an important source of care for many under-fives whose mothers are working. Domestic work is engaged in by women of any age while nannies tend to be young women in the 18–24 age group: presumably this work is done before they too have children. In this and other respects there are many parallels between the kind of domestic work they are hired to do and the position of domestic servants in the nineteenth century. In the United States where there is a high rate of female employment then domestic and child care services are largely purchased on the private market and Black and Hispanic women perform much of this work (Hewitt, 1993, p. 170). The fact that the domestic tasks in professional households are performed by women reinforces the view that these are women's work and therefore of low status.

Inequalities at Work

Unemployment tends to fall unequally on those in the lowest paid jobs, with least job security. There is a greater chance that people in low-paying and insecure jobs, the very young and the oldest in the labour force, people from ethnic or racial minorities, the disabled and handicapped will be unemployed. These workers are often non-unionized. Manufacturing homeworkers, who take out work from a supplier, are a good illustration of this process at work. Because they work in their own homes at their own pace, they are paid piece rates for the work that they do and have no protection from Health and Safety legislation. When orders decline it is a straightforward matter for the supplier to dispense with their services, knowing that if there is an upturn then, as likely as not, the homeworkers will be there again (see Allen and Wolkowitz, 1987).

There is a big difference between the pay of manual and white collar workers. The New Earnings Survey 1992 shows this in practice in table 6.1.

Although differentials in some of the better paid female occupations have reduced over the last ten years it is still the case that female earnings overall represent 80% of male (see table 6.2). Three factors are responsible: women are to be found in greater numbers in poorly paid industries, and they are in less skilled work than men; when they do do the same work as men they tend to get paid less for it; and they tend to work fewer hours than men because they do not do as much overtime (Littler and Salaman, 1984, p. 17).

Work has also to be viewed over the lifetime. Manual workers see their earnings peak quite early, reach a plateau and then decline. For middle-class workers the operation of incremental pay means that wages increase each year thus providing more security. They can plan ahead and rely on their income. The benefits offered by different jobs contribute substantially to inequalities at work: so much so that for senior executives it is not valid to take their wage as an indicator of their economic position because they usually receive many benefits in kind. The company car is the most common but there are many others, including expense accounts which enable executives to entertain at the company's expense and permit the manager a wide range of discretion over how the money is spent, while some executives obtain assistance with telephone bills, or receive clothing allowances, help with fees for private schools or share options in the company.

Accidents are another area where major inequalities in work can be

Table 6.1 Distribution of income

Full-time employees on adult rates, whose pay for the survey pay-period was not affected by absence

	Males			Females			Males and Females		
	Manual	Non-manual	All	Manual	Non-manual	All	Manual	Non-manual	All
Average gross weekly earnings (in £s) of which	268.3	400.4	340.1	170.1	256.5	241.1	250.7	334.6	304.6
overtime payments	38.0	11.8	23.8	10.3	4.8	5.8	33.0	8.6	17.3
PBR etc payments	14.8	13.2	14.0	10.8	3.2	4.6	14.1	8.6	10.6
shift etc premium payments	10.0	2.7	6.1	4.8	2.5	2.9	9.0	2.6	4.9
As percentage of average gross earnings									
overtime payments	14.1	3.0	7.0	6.1	1.9	2.4	13.2	2.6	5.7
PBR etc payments	5.5	3.3	4.1	6.4	1.3	1.9	5.6	2.6	3.5
shift etc premium payments	3.7	0.7	1.8	2.8	1.0	1.2	3.6	0.8	1.6
Distribution of gross weekly earnings (in £s)									
10 per cent earned less than	157.6	186.0	170.2	105.7	140.5	129.1	137.2	155.5	148.2
25 per cent earned less than	197.4	257.6	219.3	126.6	174.4	161.4	177.6	201.4	191.6
50 per cent earned less than	250.7	353.4	295.9	156.6	227.6	211.3	234.0	290.8	264.6
25 per cent earned more than	316.7	473.3	401.9	199.2	315.9	295.9	301.7	402.4	366.3
10 per cent earned more than	397.3	641.2	544.1	253.5	400.6	387.1	381.4	543.6	439.5

percentage earning less than

£100	0.6	0.4	0.5	6.7	0.1	2.1	1.7	0.8	1.1
£120	2.1	1.2	1.6	19.5	3.8	8.6	5.2	2.4	3.4
£150	7.8	3.9	5.6	44.7	13.7	19.2	14.4	8.3	10.5
£170	13.8	6.7	9.9	58.9	22.6	29.1	29.1	14.0	16.8
£200	26.1	12.4	18.7	75.4	38.6	45.2	34.9	24.4	28.2
£230	40.2	18.5	28.4	85.1	50.8	56.9	48.2	33.3	38.6
£270	58.3	28.1	41.9	92.6	64.0	69.1	64.4	44.5	51.6
£300	69.8	35.7	51.3	95.7	70.6	75.9	74.5	52.1	60.1
£360	84.8	51.6	66.7	98.5	82.9	85.7	87.2	65.9	73.5
£420	92.3	65.6	77.8	99.5	90.8	93.2	93.6	77.6	83.3
£480	95.9	76.3	85.3	99.9	96.0	98.7	98.6	85.3	89.4
£600	98.7	87.9	92.8	100.0	98.6	98.9	98.9	92.8	95.0
Average gross hourly earnings including overtime pay and overtime hours (p)	605	1021	807	428	690	640	576	868	750
excluding overtime pay and overtime hours (p)	589	1023	810	421	688	638	560	867	749

Source: New Earnings Survey, 1992.

Table 6.2 Women's wages as percentage of male earnings

Average gross hourly earnings, excluding the effects of overtime, full-time employees on adult rates.

| | Pence per hour | | |
	1975*	1981*	1991
ENGLAND			
Females	98.3	241.2	589.1
Males	139.3	331.2	756.9
Differential	41.0	90.0	167.8
Female earnings as a % of male earnings	70.6%	72.8%	77.8%
SCOTLAND			
Females	92.7	231.1	545.6
Males	133.8	321.3	696.4
Differential	41.1	90.2	150.8
Female earnings as a % of male earnings	69.3%	71.9%	78.3%
WALES			
Females	92.8	233.6	529.5
Males	134.9	316.4	660.8
Differential	42.1	82.8	131.3
Female earnings as a % of male earnings	68.8%	73.8%	80.1%

Source: New Earnings Survey.
* females aged 18 and over, males aged 21 and over

found: 'nearly all work deaths resulting from accidents at work are among manual workers' (Littler and Salaman, 1984, p. 22). The risk of being killed or seriously injured in an accident at work reduced over the thirty years 1965 to 1981 from 5.6 deaths and serious injuries per 100,000 employees in the UK to 2.1. This trend would now seem to have been reversed in some industries (Quick, 1991, p. 50). Critics of the government claim that the emphasis on the relaxation of controls together with the promotion of small firms has led to a more hazardous environment, for employers are more reluctant in such a tight economy to pay attention to safety measures which could increase their costs.

Disabled workers are more likely to be unemployed than able-bodied workers in the UK. The overall unemployment rate for disabled workers in the mid-1980s was three times higher for disabled men as it was for their able-bodied counterparts. For women it was more than double. The respective figures were: men 27% (11%), women 20% (9%) – the figures in brackets are for the able-bodied (Martin et al., 1989, p. 74). The Department of Employment operates a quota scheme for disabled people in order to increase their chances of work. This stipulates that employers with twenty or more employees have a duty to employ at least 3 per cent of their workforce from the ranks of the registered disabled. Yet less than one third of employers fulfil their quota and it is a small minority of disabled people who are registered disabled: in 1985 20% of men and 8% of women (p. 74).

Class and racial inequalities are reflected in work. It is manual workers who are most likely to succumb to illness and disease while the unemployed population has poorer health than those who are in work. Research studies have shown that the fact of unemployment can cause a deterioration in mental health and there is some evidence to link physical ill-health and suicide with unemployment, although causality has not been proven (Whitehead, 1987, p. 22). Stress and psychological problems are a well-documented result of unemployment (Fagin, 1984). Racial inequality is seen in the incidence and distribution of unemployment. Writing about the position in the mid-1980s Jenkins reported that the unemployment rate for white workers was half that for ethnic minorities, and that 'The situation of young workers is most severe: 16 per cent of economically active young white people between 16 and 24 years were unemployed, compared to 33 per cent of ethnic minorities' (Jenkins, in Gallie, 1988, p. 314). Because of the structural changes in the British economy – the major shift from manufacturing to service industries – the ethnic minority population who have settled in certain areas in large numbers, for example, West Yorkshire, West Midlands and the North West, are in parts of the country where unemployment rates are high: around two to three times those for whites (Ward and Cross, in Brown and Scase, 1991, p. 119).

Long Term Unemployment

A particular feature of the mass unemployment which developed from the late 1970s was the reappearance of long term unemployment. Given the wholesale closures of industries in certain regions of the country this was perhaps inevitable for older workers, who, thrown out of work in their fifties, might never obtain a job again. What was new in the late 1970s and the 1980s was the appearance of long term unemployment among the young. Government training schemes for all unemployed youngsters under the age of eighteen have attempted to mitigate the effect of this unemployment, but of course these are not *real jobs* and cannot act as a substitute for them. Demoralization of young people resulting from unemployment has been a real fear. Recent outbreaks of rioting and looting led by young people might suggest that this was the case among some sectors and some parts of the country. Hutson and Jenkins, in their study of unemployment among young people in Swansea, found that demoralization had not resulted because to a greater or lesser extent in the three areas that they studied the experience of unemployment was understood through a predominantly individualist framework which accorded responsibility for their position to the young people themselves (1989).

William Beveridge's great report of 1942 *Social Insurance and Allied Services*, which laid the foundations of the post-war welfare state originated as a report to the government on the rationalization of the existing unemployment and sickness benefit schemes. Beveridge transformed this limited brief into a blueprint for social security, at the heart of which lay the commitment by the state to provide full employment. This underpinned the post-war development of the welfare state because it ensured that large numbers of people would be freed from the uncertainty and hopelessness characteristic of high unemployment. With the onset of deindustrialization the conditions for full employment would seem to have disappeared: now it seems that the state no longer has the power to effect full employment. The structural changes in the economy which have ended millions of manufacturing jobs have ushered in a new era of mass unemployment where in the 1980s the unemployment rate never fell below 7 per cent. The manufacturing job loss had been so extensive that it is difficult to see how an equivalent number of jobs in the service sector could be created.

The problems have multiplied since the onset of mass unemployment. The social security system was based on the assumption, contained in the Beveridge Report, that there would be full employment. Unemployment benefit was designed to be paid for a short period while a person was looking for work and not to be a benefit for those who were long term unemployed. The cut-off after a year means that a decreasing number of unemployed people receive the benefit: in the first quarter of 1993 only 23.9 per cent of the unemployed received unemployment benefit (DSS, 1993). The social security budget accounts for around a third of public expenditure and is the most costly social policy area. Unsurprisingly, government has been looking to ways of reducing this and various proposals have been mooted, among them the reduction of unemployment benefit from twelve months to six months, after which a person would have to draw Social Assistance. Another is Workfare – the stipulation that claimants should do voluntary work in return for their benefit.

Older Workers

It is among older workers that the reappearance of long-term unemployment has been most acutely felt. The restructuring of the British economy has meant that certain workers have less bargaining power than they once had. In this category we can put the older workers, those workers over the age of 50. The figures below show the extent to which there has been decreasing participation in the labour force by older workers (Laczko and Phillipson, 1991, p. 2).

Labour force participation rate (percentages)

Men aged 55–9

1965	1970	1975	1980	1985	1988
95.7	95.3	93.0	90.1	81.8	81.6

Men aged 60–4

89.2	86.7	82.3	71.2	54.5	55.1

Men aged 65 and over

23.7	20.1	15.6	10.3	8.2	7.7

Since the onset of mass unemployment early retirement from the labour market has become a regular occurrence for older workers. This has been caused by a decline in the number of semi-skilled and unskilled jobs, the increase in the number of women workers in the economy, the fact that occupational pension schemes make provision for early retirement and the additional number of workers who choose early retirement as an alternative to full time work (Laczko and Phillipson, p. 19). Whether older workers should continue in the labour market is directly related to the labour supply and most recently they have been treated as workers who can be dispensed with before others. Once they are unemployed then older workers are far less likely to gain work again. Ageism, discrimination against older workers, is a factor here with some employers discounting the value of workers in this age group. The resulting big growth in early retirement has meant a burden on the state as many workers under retirement age have to claim state benefits.

Part Time Work

The growth of part time work has been a key change in the British labour market in the late twentieth century. Britain has one of the highest percentages of part timers in the European Community: 90 per cent of those who classed themselves as part time in 1985 were women and of these 82 per cent were married women (Hurstfield, 1987). But increasingly part time work is being done by groups of the workforce who in the past would have worked full time, for instance, there has been a big growth in part time work among the 16–19 age group (1987). Part timers are now a central feature of the employment strategy of many firms and large parts of the public sector. What growth there has been in the labour market in the 1980s has been in the part time sector. Among the part time work force in 1990 86 per cent were women and 71 per cent of these did not want a full time job (CSO, 1992, p. 77). Part time work has advantages for the employee and the employer: for the worker it enables her to fit in work with other household and family commitments such as child care or caring for an elderly or sick member of the family; while for the employer the part timer is valued because given the hours that she works there is no requirement that National Insurance contributions be paid and the worker is outside much employment legislation.

Retailing is one of the biggest employers of part timers, as fully 45 per cent of the retailing workforce are now part timers. One of the attractions of the part timer to the retailer is the fact that they can be used to bridge the gap between the full timers' working week of 39 hours and the 80 plus hours that many supermarkets now operate. In retailing we see the clearest example of another social change in the labour market, the rise of part time student working. Hutson estimated on the basis of a study carried out in Swansea that across the country between 60 and 80 per cent of sixth formers are doing regular part time work while at school or college, with this usually taking the form of a 'Saturday job' (1990). This part time work carries on at university and for some students is an important part of their income.

There is some disquiet about children working below the age of sixteen. This often will begin with the paper round but there is plenty of evidence to suggest that some children are working much longer hours than the seven or eight a week occupied by a paper round: there are reports of children working thirty hours a week or more for very low pay (Hobbs et al., 1992). As with other kinds of part time work the pressure for this to expand is twofold: the youngsters want the work because it enables them to be a little more independent of their parents at a time when they are increasingly interested in clothes, cassettes and entertainment, while for some employers child employment represents a cheap and very flexible form of labour. Part time work can also be viewed as a form of work experience and for many parents it is obviously a boost to the family income if teenagers are buying their own clothes rather than getting the money from their parents. In the past the law has taken a protectionist stance towards child labour, seeing it as something which should be strictly controlled and regulated. For example, the 1973 Employment of Children Act required all workers under sixteen to be registered with the DHSS, banned children from working between the hours of 7 pm and 7 am and limited hours of work to two on school days. The fact that this Act has never been implemented would seem to suggest that governments recognize that to do so would be very unpopular.

The Feminization of the Work Force

Two trends stand out among changes in work patterns in the period since 1945: the increasing number of women in the workforce and the expansion in the number of part time jobs. They are related, for 88 per cent of all part time workers in 1988 were women and approximately 45 per cent of employed women are in part time work (Dex, in Gallie, 1988, p. 297). The number of women in the workforce increased from 6.7 million in 1948 to 9.2 million in 1980 (Morris, in Gallie, p. 377). Married women account for a much larger share of the female work-force than they used to: 30 per cent in 1951 and in 1984 69 per cent (Morris, in Gallie). The attraction of part time work for many women is that they can fit it around household and child care responsibilities. It would appear that work is becoming more of a form of identity for certain groups in the female workforce, particularly those who are in professional jobs, and this is probably related to the diminished status of motherhood and child care in our society.

Along with their increased participation in the labour force many women would seem to have a changed attitude to the home and domestic work. In the nineteenth century the trend was for working-class women to leave the labour force: in 1851 only 25 per cent of wives were not in paid employment whereas in 1911 it had climbed to 90 per cent. Over this period there was a growing belief among women that the role of housewife was a good option which would give women a secure identity within the family and to this end working-class women strove to remove the taint of domestic service from household tasks. Emancipation was seen as a move away from paid work towards caring for the home and the family (Bourke, forthcoming; Roberts, 1988).

But what has led to this diminished status for motherhood in our society? In some ways it may not be a change in the status of motherhood so much as a change in the values of the population relating to income and standard of living. The dominant message of the culture is to be a consumer and couples who have small children and mortgages are encouraged by advertising to acquire a range of consumer durables. Many people will have obtained these on credit so the birth of the first child or subsequent children will mean a problem in paying off this debt. The culture encourages us not to wait for goods by saving but instead to buy these goods and then pay for them via the credit system. The status of housework has declined while the time devoted to such important tasks has also diminished. Cooking has become for many families a much speedier process, using precooked convenience foods and utilizing the technology of the freezer and the microwave. Clothes making and mending – traditionally an important part of the housewife's role – has declined. Naturally food retailers are keen to promote convenience foods because of the higher profit margins there are on these goods while clothes manufacturers are anxious to encourage the public to acquire new clothes rather than 'make do and mend'. But time is another important consideration, for if both partners in a marriage are working full time then there is little time left for these activities. The strains in families with both parents working full time are more easily negotiated by professionals whose income allows them to purchase domestic and child-care support and services. The spill-over of stress from work to home has been remarked upon and this can lead to marital problems. In a 1980s survey it was shown that during the first ten years of marriage each additional year of full employment increased the odds of divorce by 6 per cent (Ermisch, quoted in McRae, 1989, p. 3). The contemporary appeal of the workplace for women lies not just in financial reward but in the social contacts which it furnishes.

Homeworking

The traditional image of the homeworker is a woman working for low wages, with no employment protection, no security of employment, isolated from other workers and not a member of a trade union. Yet the majority of homeworkers do not fit this description: it applies to manufacturing homeworkers who work for the textile industry or make toys or other products at piece rates. As long ago as 1971 they were in the minority among homeworkers, clerical homeworkers being twice as numerous even then, and are now being outnumbered by the latest homeworkers, the teleworkers, who can work at home because of the computer which connects them to the office. There is a great range of occupations to be found among the ranks of the homeworkers covering nearly all occupational groups (Hakim, in Pahl, 1988, p. 615). Their numbers have greatly increased as they tend to be part time workers and this form of work has seen a big expansion in the last twenty years. Two thirds of women home-workers, excluding childminders, work less than sixteen hours a week. This means that their earnings are typically low. Hakim makes a distinction between *people who work at home* and *people who work at home or from home as a base*. Among the first category it is women who predominate – 71 per cent – and men predominate in the second category – again at 71 per cent (p. 614). There is a clear sexual division operating which is manifested in the rewards of homeworkers: they are among the highest paid workers in the country (men) and they are among the lowest (women), The big increase in women's participation in the labour force has been in the realm of part time jobs. Conventionally part time employment is work which does not occupy more than twenty-seven hours a week.

Many of the problems of homeworkers stem from the fact that employers have been able to dictate poor conditions of work. This does not apply to certain categories of executives or professionals who, because of their position in the company or a particular skill which they possess, will be able to have a more equal relationship. Overall, however, the social relations of production are dictated by the employers because they give out the work.

Teleworking – the use of a computer which enables work to be done at home – is a growth sector: it has long been hyped by the media and by IT gurus like Alvin Toffler, with his vision of the electronic cottage where the worker can work at the computer, then get up, open the door and commune with nature. This is the traditional dream of a rural idyll, with roses growing round the door, low ceilings and pine kitchen but with one addition, the computer terminal linked to the head office. The proponents of teleworking speak enthusiastically of the other benefits this style of life offers: no commuting means time saved from the daily traffic jam; in aggregate

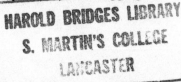

this means less pollution and energy saving; because the computer can be used at any time then if the worker wants to take the day off then s/he can do so as they can work at their computer any time of the day or night. Employers should welcome the idea, its proponents argue, as it means that they can dispense with the fixed costs of offices with their property values and maintenance costs. Its value to women who have the care of children has been mentioned but it will also be attractive to disabled people who will welcome the chance to contribute to the world of work in this way. Older workers who have been made redundant in their fifties might also find teleworking attractive in those years before they can draw their pension. So much for the dream but what is the reality?

Teleworking is certainly growing: this is not in dispute, although not at the rate that was forecast in the past. British Telecom estimated in 1974 that as many as 13.5 million workers could be teleworkers in the UK by the 1990s but the most recent, and more sober, prediction is that there will be between 2.5 and 3.3 million teleworkers by the mid-1990s (*Independent*, 7 April 1992). Teleworking would seem most likely to occur in industries which already have a high IT component: banking, insurance and retailing as well as amongst freelance professionals who are acting as consultants.

Teleworking can take two forms: it can mean that there is a direct communications link between the home computer and the office, usually via a modem, or it can simply mean that the worker works at home using the computer and then takes a floppy disk to work where the material is processed. On the whole, the most common form of teleworking is where there is a link between the home and the workplace, as in various forms of data entry or data processing. The more independent professional workers, whose work does not involve them in such large scale processing of data, would be the ones to take the disk to work or merely put it in the post. The automation of the office could well mean in the future that more clerical workers do this kind of work from home. There are clear dangers here: the collective forms of organization which workers have evolved through time in the shape of trade unions will be lost and the social contact and social life which many people value about work, sometimes more than the salary, will also disappear. Companies will be much more able to dispense with the services of clerical workers who may well find this work isolating. In sum, teleworking can be viewed from this perspective as part of a deskilling process which has been gathering pace in office work for some time.

Korte's survey of 117 teleworkers in Britain and West Germany in

1987 found that flexibility – defined as the ability to work when it suits one – was the most important advantage. Others in order of importance were: the ability to combine family and child care with work, the ability to meet the demands of the family, the ability to combine other activities with their work and the end of commuting problems (Korte, in van Rijn and Williams, 1988, p. 385).

What are we to make of this trend? It reinforces the claim that the home is an increasingly important part of life. Think of it: one need never leave the home if one's work is there, one can be more than adequately entertained there. It could mean that in the future, if travelling to work by car becomes environmentally prohibitive then the country commuters can stay tight in their rural fastness – and the suburbanites in their leafy avenues – with the help of their computer. More immediately, it can offer the prospect of work for certain groups who find it difficult to enter the labour market: as we have seen it will be appealing to women who have the care of their children, although one cannot do a teleworking job at the same time as looking after the children and at least one firm in this country expects its teleworkers to make proper arrangements for childcare (Wilson, 1991, p. 47). Teleworking opens up possibilities for disabled people to enter employment, because with specially developed software more of them could do paid work. There would seem to be a role here for regulation by the state as well, otherwise it becomes comparatively easy for isolated homeworkers, in clerical occupations, to see their wages forced down by employers as they will have few alternatives to this form of work, especially if they are disabled or occupy a weak labour market position.

One of the key themes of Thatcherism in the 1980s was the need for the British to rediscover their entrepreneurial spirit, and they were encouraged to do this by the inducements to start small businesses: in the mid-1980s there were over 299 government initiatives to help small businesses (Burrows and Curran, in Cross and Payne, 1991, p. 20). The opportunities for other kinds of work being done from home are less straightforward – the computer or word processor only requires a desk or a table top but someone who wanted to repair cars from home obviously requires a garage and some hardstanding for the repair of the vehicles, not always available in built-up residential districts. Other small businesses are likely to require quite a deal of space. If someone is selling products from home – such as plastic kitchen ware or children's books – then they need storage space. For some kinds of business operated from home, such as a man doing carpentry from a workshop built in his back garden, then there are planning requirements to be complied with not to mention the neighbours who may well object if there is too much noise! The psychological separation of paid employment from home, although it is less than two hundred years old, is nonetheless valued by many people who welcome the chance to shut off from work when they get home. The danger of homework is that it is ever-present and conversely, as mothers of small children find when they are homeworking, family needs intrude into the work and stop it getting done!

Caring

Caring is a form of homework but because it has traditionally been part of a woman's work in the home has not been identified as a separate category until quite recently. In the 1980s 'carer' entered the dictionary for the first time, a recognition that it is now generally accepted as an occupation. Caring can take a variety of forms: most commonly it is found in everyday life in the ordinary tasks of cleaning, cooking and assistance that one person gives to another. The contribution of carers to the physical, social and emotional care of many groups who otherwise would have been reliant on the health and social services is now widely acknowledged. The White Paper *Caring for People*, which led to the reorganization of health and social services in the NHS and Community Care Act 1990, remarked that:

> the reality is that most care is provided by family, friends and neighbours. The majority of carers take on these responsibilities willingly, but the Government recognises that many need help to be able to manage what can become a heavy burden. Their lives can be made much easier if the right support is there at the right time, and a key responsibility of statutory service providers should be to do all they can to assist and support carers. (Department of Health, 1990)

Although Social Services Departments involve carers' organizations in the discussion and planning of services the finance for adequate support services has not been forthcoming from central government. Caring for many people is an isolating and monotonous daily routine with scarce opportunity to get out of the house. 'Respite' care for the dependant which allows this is in short supply.

The 1984 General Household Survey identified about six million carers in Great Britain and 1.4 million of these spent more than twenty hours a week on the caring task (Social Services Committee, 1990, p. vii). The point made often enough is that if these people were not doing this work then the burden would fall upon the state and the cost would be enormous: a 1990 estimate put the figure at somewhere between £15 billion and £24 billion (Family Policy Studies Centre, 1989). The GHS survey found that of those carers below pensionable age only about half were in paid employment: 32 per cent were in full time work, 14 per cent were in part time work while 54 per cent were not in paid work (Social Services Committee, 1990, p. vii). There is only one benefit specifically for this important group of people: the Invalid Care Allowance. This is only paid to a carer if the person they are looking after is able to claim the Attendance Allowance. The carer must have to provide care for thirty-five hours a week. A person can claim the ICA while working part time but they are only allowed to earn £20 a week before money is deducted from their benefit. It was the carers who were not working at all who were most likely to fall below the poverty line (Evandrou, 1990, p. 27).

The end of full employment has meant many changes in the perception of the problem of unemployment. Between 1945 and 1975 there was a national consensus that full employment was the norm and that mass unemployment was something which belonged to the past. Both assumptions are no longer valid. Keynesian demand management of the economy could not cope with the twin crises of high unemployment and high inflation from the 1970s onwards. Innumerable schemes were started by Labour and Conservative governments to cope with the problem of mass unemployment, principally focused on the need for the provision of training for young people. This was in response to the fact that the labour market had changed greatly over the last twenty years, with the number of apprenticeships declining massively. What had also declined was the number of jobs in manufacturing industry which of course were largely for male manual workers. In their place new jobs were created in the service sector of the economy but these tended on the whole to be clerical and secretarial and often were of a part time nature – in short, they were jobs for women and so we have seen another big change, namely, the feminization of the labour force, with almost all the new jobs being created of a part time nature.

Existing analyses in the sociology of work were premissed on the basis that the workforce was overwhelmingly male with women's work being seen as peripheral to the main business of earning a living. Pahl proposed a new understanding of work decisions and behaviour, namely, the household work strategy. In the household work strategy both partners decide the extent of the commitment to the labour market and the extent of the commitment to child care and the work of the home. In doing so Pahl is proposing that we look on work in the way that it was regarded in the pre-industrial era where both husband and wife and the children were involved in the labour of the household. As he remarks, up to the industrial period the male worker would often have a secondary occupation, a craftsman for instance might well do agricultural work. Pahl and others have emphasized the importance of the great amount of work that is performed in the home: the care of children being a major activity in many households, the everyday work of running the home, the cleaning and the cooking, the maintenance of the home. With the last category Pahl shows how there has been a big increase in the amount of what he and Gershuny term 'self-provisioning', the do-it-yourself work that is carried on by households because of their ownership of electric drills and other equipment, although this needs to be balanced by the decline in the time spent on tasks such as cooking and clothes making.

Pahl's ideas were generated from his study of work on the Isle of Sheppey in Kent. Based on this work he came to the conclusion that there were two types of household: the 'work-rich' and the 'work-poor'. The 'work-rich' household has multiple opportunities for employment, typically both husband and wife will be in employment and many may also have secondary jobs which will be possible because of the range of contacts which they have. Sometimes, this work will not be declared to the tax authorities, 'moonlighting'. Then there are work-starved households where the chief wage earner will be unemployed and the operation of the benefit system only allows the wife to earn a very small amount before it is deducted from their social security. The work-starved do not have the contacts which would enable them to obtain extra work which they could do illegally, and they would be frightened of their neighbours reporting this employment to the social security. Because they are poor from living on benefit for so long they do not have the tools which would enable them to do self-provisioning work. Jordan et al. (1992) made a study of families living in poverty in Exeter in order to research the life worlds or assumptions about the world held by poor families. They found that these families were not work-starved but rather they combined work with work in the black economy, that it to say it was not declared, or they combined unemployment and the receipt of social security benefits with this informal economy work. There was a clear majority view that the social security rules which meant that a claimant can only receive a very small part of this income were unfair and hence there was no moral reason why they should not be disregarded. Again, several men in their study reported that they used their period of unemployment to redecorate the house.

Interestingly, there had been no change in the view of the breadwinner role. Indeed, in the one household where the man was at home and the woman was in full time work then 'Mr Wye still defines himself as a worker and a provider, and Mrs Wye still sees her first responsibility as to care for the children' (Jordan et al., 1992, p. 14). The authors summarized their findings on the sexual division of labour: 'The man's obligation to do paid work is binding, the woman's elective; in the case of unpaid work the reverse is the case' (p. 16). The extent to which this view is holding up across occupational groups and across the country is difficult to determine. There has been some evidence in the past to support the feminist contention that women who work full time are also expected by their partners to do the bulk of domestic work with the result that they are in fact working a 'double shift' at work and at home. Recently, however, Gershuny has questioned whether this is still such a strong feature of the domestic organization of labour. Using diaries which list the time spent on various household tasks he found that husbands of full time employed wives increased their time on cooking and cleaning from twenty minutes to forty minutes per average day (Gershuny, in Abercrombie and Warde, 1992, p. 86).

The present social security system organized around the principle of work is seen by many commentators to be unsuited to the post-full employment society which Britain has become. There is growing support for what is called Citizens' Income – or Basic Income – which is a weekly payment payable to all adults in the society. There would be no eligibility test for this payment whatsoever. The advantages claimed for this proposal are that it would enable certain groups of workers to be rewarded whereas at present they are not – carers, houseworkers etc. Those people who did not take part in the formal economy of waged work could then make a decision as to whether they wanted to supplement their Citizens' Income with a paid job. In this way it is hoped that various low paying jobs would become attractive as the wage would be a supplement and not regarded as the sole source of income. The advantage of this proposal is that it does away with the bureaucracy needed to administer the means-tested social security system. Because it is based on individual citizens as being the unit of entitlement the Citizens' Income removes the present system's stipulation that couples' joint income should be taken into account when assessing means tested benefits (see Parker, 1989).

The welfare state consensus of the thirty year period after the end of the Second World War was premissed upon full employment which meant, in fact, full time employment. The twin processes of the feminization of the work force and the big increase in part time working would seem to demand a new response. Part time work which allows time for child care and other responsbilities seems to fit better with the expectations of many people today (Hewitt, 1993). We have seen how this distribution of work has broken down in the last twenty years but the social security system has not really responded to this. The onset of high unemployment has produced a flurry of schemes to provide training for youngsters who are vulnerable to unemployment. But more than that, work has assumed even greater prominence across a range of policies. In education, the emphasis on preparation for work is reflected throughout the curriculum and most school students now do 'work experience'. In higher education the government's *Enterprise in Higher Education* programme is designed to accentuate those features of university study which will make students more 'enterprising' and thus better employees.

Yet the economy is not producing sufficient jobs to sustain this preoccupation with paid work. Meanwhile other vital work is not done – looking after public parks, cleaning the streets, caring for sick and elderly people – because there is insufficient funding to pay for it. It seems only a matter of time before we realize that our preoccupation with paid work is a block on the useful employment of millions of our fellow citizens. The challenge facing society in the late twentieth century is to move to a new understanding of the relationship between work and income in which full time paid work is not given the overriding importance that it has enjoyed up until now. Social policy needs to ensure that the existing inequalities in the distribution of work are not reproduced in the new forms of work which will dominate in the next century.

Discussion Questions

1 'The male organization of working time is incompatible with the care of children and other dependants' (Patricia Hewitt). Do you agree with this statement?

2 Is a statutory retirement age an example of ageism?

Further Reading

Duncan Gallie (ed.), *Employment in Britain* (Oxford: Blackwell, 1988) is a key collection of articles, as is Ray Pahl, *On Work* (Blackwell, 1988). Patricia Hewitt, *About Time* (London: 1993) is a stimulating discussion of feminization and part time working which explores policy implications.

References

Abercrombie, N and Warde, A (1992), *Social Change in Contemporary Britain*, Cambridge: Polity Press.

Allen, S and Wolkowitz, C (1987), *Homeworking: myths and realities*, London: Macmillan.

Bourke, J (forthcoming), 'How to be happy though married: housewifery in working-class Britain, 1860–1914', *Past and Present*.

Brown, P and Scase, R (1991), *Poor Work: Disadvantage and the Division of Labour*, Milton Keynes: Open University Press.

Burrows, R and Curran, J (1991), 'Not such a small business; reflections on the rhetoric, the reality and the future of the Enterprise Culture', in M Cross, and G Payne (eds), *Work and the Enterprise Culture*, London: Falmer Press.

Central Statistical Office (1992), *Social Trends, 22*, London: HMSO.

Department of Health (1990), *Caring for People*, London: HMSO.

Department of Social Security (1993), *Quarterly Analysis of Unemployed Claimants*, Government Statistical Service, May.

Evandrou, M (1990), *Challenging the Invisibility of Carers: Mapping Informal Care Nationally*, London School of Economics: Welfare State Programme Discussion Paper 49.

Fagin, L (1984), *The Forsaken Families: the effects of unemployment on family life*, Harmondsworth: Penguin.

Family Policy Studies Centre (1989), *Family Policy Bulletin, 6*, Winter.

Gallie, D (ed.) (1988), *Employment in Britain*, Oxford: Blackwell.

Heelas, P and Morris, P (1992), *The Values of the Enterprise Culture*, London: Routledge.

Hewitt, P (1993), *About Time: the revolution in work and family life*, London: Institute of Public Policy Research/Rivers Oram Press.

Hobbs, S, Lavalette, M and McKechnie, J (1992), 'The emerging problem of child labour', *Critical Social Policy, 34*, Summer.

House of Commons Social Services Committee (1990), *Fifth Report: Community Care: Carers*, Session 1989–90, London: HMSO.

Hurstfield, J (1987), *Part-timers under Pressure: paying the price of flexibility*, London: Low Pay Unit.

Hutson, S (1990), 'Saturday jobs: sixth formers earning and spending', unpublished paper, British Sociological Association conference.

Hutson, S and Jenkins, R (1989), *Taking the Strain: families, unemployment and the transition to adulthood*, Milton Keynes: Open University Press.

Jordan, B, James, S, Kay, H and Redley, M (1992), *Trapped in Poverty? Labour Market Decisions in Low Income Households*, London: Routledge.

Keat, R and Abercrombie, N (eds) (1991), *Enterprise Culture*, London: Routledge.

Laczko, F and Phillipson, C (1991), *Changing Work and Retirement*, Milton Keynes: Open University Press.

Littler, C R and Salaman, G (1984), *Class at Work: the design, allocation and control of jobs*, London: Batsford.

McRae, S (1989), *Family Working Time and Family Life*, London: Policy Studies Institute.

Martin, J, White, A and Meltzer, H (1988), *Disabled Adults: services, transport and employment*, London: OPCS.

Pahl, R E (1984), *Divisions of Labour*, Oxford: Basil Blackwell.

Pahl, R E (ed.) (1988), *On Work: historical, comparative and theoretical approaches*, Oxford: Basil Blackwell.

Parker, H (1989), *Instead of the Dole*, London: Routledge.

Postgate, R (1984), *Home: a place for work?*, London: Calouste Gulbenkian Foundation.

Quick, A (1991), *Unequal Risks: accidents and social policy*, London: Socialist Health Association.

Roberts, E (1988), *Women's Work 1840–1940*, London: Macmillan.

van Rijn, F and Williams, R (1988), *Concerning Home Telematics*, North Holland: Elsevier.

Whitehead, M (1987), *The Health Divide: inequalities in health in the 1980s*, London: Health Education Council.

Wilson, A (1991), *Teleworking – Flexibility for a Few*, Falmer: Institute of Manpower Studies, University of Sussex.

7

PLAYING

Despite the rupture in the post-war consensus on welfare both Conservative and Labour governments have agreed since the mid-1970s on the need for a role for the state in the provision of leisure. Government has over the years established various public bodies which have, as part of their remit, the requirement to seek and provide for the leisure needs of the population: among them can be listed the Arts Council, the Countryside Commission and the Sports Council, although the biggest expenditure on leisure comes through the medium of local government. Despite this state involvement leisure is dominated by commercial interests and a large voluntary sector. Although there is more leisure time now than ever before as the time spent on paid work has declined in the twentieth century, people are retiring earlier and have longer holidays, leisure is, like the other areas of social life, characterized by inequalities of gender, age and social class. If leisure consists in one famous definition of making love, drinking, watching television, then much of social life can be described as leisure (Roberts, 1978). It can also be argued that some of working life cannot easily be divorced from leisure because there are opportunities for social contact which are 'non-work'. Leisure is experienced differentially in our society – it is a common observation that men make a clean break with their work when they come home while many women, even if they are at paid work during the day, find themselves often doing two activities at once, e.g. knitting, mending or ironing while watching television. The chapters on Viewing, Shopping and to some extent Travelling also dealt with important aspects of leisure experience but this chapter explores the extent to which government policy can and should meet the leisure needs of the population. After a brief historical account of the growth of leisure the mixed economy of leisure is explored and then the leisure opportunities for two groups – women and unemployed people – are examined.

The separation of work and leisure is a product of industrialization. Before the industrial revolution there was a unity between work and leisure and recreation based on the household economy, where the entire family would be engaged in the same kind of work, whether that be in the fields or the spinning or weaving of cloth. The nineteenth century was dominated by the idea of work to an extent that is unimaginable now. The only day of rest was Sunday and even recreation on a Sunday was strictly governed by certain rules and regulations which varied in their application from one part of the country to another, but, in effect, meant that all places of public entertainment – pubs, music halls, theatres, football grounds – were closed. The first breakthrough for working people was the granting of the half day holiday on Saturday afternoons which, among other things, enabled men to attend football matches. Although hours were long, work was not continuous all day and everyday and there were some recreational opportunities, for men at least, including going to the pub on weekday evenings. In many working-class communities, indeed, the pub was the centre point of activity and thus it became a focus for those who wished to change working-class habits of recreation. Temperance reformers set their sights on breaking the link between the pub and recreation. They offered alternatives to the public house – among them coffee taverns – and the late nineteenth century saw the birth of organizations such as the Young Men's Christian Association (YMCA) and other societies designed to stimulate the discussion of political and religious ideas. Churches were particularly active in the provision of recreation for the working class, hoping, in part, to capture new attenders for their services. Some of the most long lasting expressions of this church-based recreational activity were the new football clubs that were created from the 1870s, some of which have survived as Football League clubs today.

The forms that working-class recreation took in the last century were part of a wider debate about what kind of society was being created. Commercial interests were naturally very active, trying to attract the working-class market whether that be the betting shop, the music hall or the new tabloid press from the 1890s. Some forms can be seen to start in one sector and end in another: football clubs started in the religious/voluntary sector and then became part of the commercial sector. Nonetheless the working class in the nineteenth century remained true to their name. Their work was often to enable a 'leisure class' of wealthy middle-class people to pursue a life almost entirely devoted to leisure. Domestic service still employed substantial numbers of women until the First World War.

It was in the nineteenth century that the state became involved in recreational provision. The designation of parks and open spaces for the workers in industrial towns was prompted by the fear of disease spreading if workers did not get some fresh air in their lungs. Thus the large parks, the pride of many cities, must be seen as related to the public health reforms of the last century (Coalter et al., 1988). As has been remarked, from the mid-nineteenth century the role of the state in leisure provision was generally to allow local authorities to take advantage of the generosity of local philanthropists by spending some money themselves on these facilities, as with the Museums Act 1849, the Public Libraries Act 1850 and the Recreation Grounds Act 1852 (Henry, 1993).

The improvement in the economic position of the working class, which occurred after the First World War, was to give many people the opportunity to enjoy leisure and recreation in a way that their forebears would not have dreamed possible. Cinema, radio, dance halls, rambling and cycling were just some of the leisure pursuits which took up their spare time. In 1938 the passing of the Holidays with Pay Act meant that every employer had to give the workforce one week's paid holiday a year. After the Second World War holidays away from home – interrupted by the emergency conditions of the war – began again. Holiday camps became a very popular way of spending a holiday, broadening their appeal from the middle class to the working class. The emergence of the mass ownership of the motor car by the 1960s brought mobility to the family holiday. No longer were people content to spend a week in one location at a guest house; instead they would drive to a seaside town from where they would drive out to other 'beauty spots'.

But a larger scale mobility was to affect the British holiday industry much more profoundly – the package holiday, taking large numbers of people abroad at cheap rates to stay in hotels and soak up the sun – and the most popular destination was Spain, where the mass migration of sun seekers from Britain each year began to alter the character of the Costas, making parts of them more akin to Margate or Blackpool in a heat wave. Each year even further destinations have been sought out so that, with the easy accessibility afforded by air travel, almost the entire world is within reach of the tourist. Destinations which previously were 'out of bounds' now become affordable for the mass tourist by means of a package – India, China,

Africa. Tourism on this scale then begins to affect the culture and economy of many societies importing Western values and mores. Yet the glossy brochures disguise the fact that the holiday package promotional literature is aimed at white, heterosexual couples often with children. Ethnic minorities are seldom ever portrayed as holiday makers (Urry, 1990, p. 142).

The holiday is the most obvious form of non-work, defined by the leisure statisticians as more than four nights spent away from home. Over the last twenty years the pattern of holiday making has changed greatly in the UK. In the early 1970s only 18 per cent of holidays were taken abroad with the rest taken in the UK (Gratton and Taylor, 1977, p. 36). By 1984 the number of foreign holidays had doubled and by 1990 the total number of holidays taken by British residents had reached a total of 20.5 million (Central Statistical Office, 1992, p. 184). Figure 7.1 shows the clear relationship between social class and holiday making.

This clear association between social class and holiday making is an instance of the way in which social inequalities reproduce themselves in the sphere of leisure. In his book *Poverty in the United Kingdom* Peter Townsend claimed that 'Two or three weeks summer holiday away from home is another social revolution of the mid-twentieth century which, now that it has become a majority convention, adds to the needs which the average family is expected to meet' (Townsend, 1979, p. 52). As we can see from figure 7.1, 58 per cent of social classes D and E did not take a holiday in 1990. This is a facet of leisure deprivation – the same people will be disadvantaged in many other ways, not least by their lack of access to some of the recreation activities provided by the public and private sector.

Playing at Home

In the Victorian era, and on into the inter-war years, the working-class home was somewhere to escape *from* if one wanted to enjoy one's leisure hours. Men would go to the local pub in large numbers, hence the existence of so many small corner of the street public houses. For the working-class woman, home was a place of work and drudgery without the domestic applicances which seem so essential to us or the domestic servants which were so much a part of her middle-class sister's life. Cooking and cleaning were time consuming processes which did not permit women very much time for recreation, though the inter-war years did see the improvement of

Figure 7.1 Number of holidays[1] per year by social class

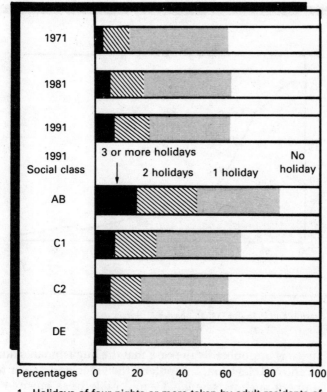

Percentages   0   20   40   60   80   100

1   Holidays of four nights or more taken by adult residents of
Great Britain in Great Britain and abroad.
Source: British National Travel Survey, British Tourist Authority,
cited in *Social Trends*, 23, 1993.

domestic conditions with the introduction of some new appliances.
The mass ownership of the wireless set and the gramophone in the
1930s marked the beginning of the era of home entertainment. Cherry
writes: 'There was a boom in consumer goods for the home, where
there was a sharp rise in household expenditure. In spite of the fact
that by 1939 only 8.5 out of 12.6 million homes had been wired for
electricity, radios and electric irons had entered into half this total,
and vacuum cleaners into a quarter' (Cherry, 1984, pp. 41–2). But it
was television which ensured the triumph of the home in the contest
to supply the mass entertainment needs of the British public. This can
be seen from figure 7.2 which shows the huge fall in cinema
attendance over the period from 1951 to 1984.

Figure 7.2 Average weekly cinema admissions, 1951–84

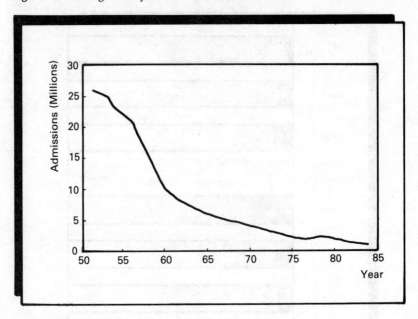

Source: C Gratton and P Taylor (1987), *Leisure in Britain*.

Nowadays it is undoubtedly the case that the Englishman's home is his leisure centre. Television, computers, the video and newer forms of entertainment such as satellite TV and cable have ensured this. Men and women spend over half their leisure time in the home (Glyptis and Chambers, 1982, p. 248). The television is the means by which we can watch videos, play computer games and entertain ourselves with CD Rom. Of course people do a lot more than watch television in their homes: it is the centre for a multitude of activities. At certain times in an individual's life the home will be more important than at others. Children under ten will be, apart from school time, mainly in and around the home whilst the onset of teenage sees youngsters increasingly spending their spare time away from home. Families with young children tend to be very home centred, although as family size increases then the need for space increases and the actual available space diminishes. In these circumstances in the past the street was a convenient and safe place for most children to play; with the large increase in the number of cars this is, sadly, no longer the case. The growing trend for women to be in paid employment has meant that there are many fewer people around in residential areas during the day and this can produce isolation for those who are at home. There have been reports of elderly people who live with relations voluntarily going into old people's homes because of the lack of company during the day – both their children are at work and the grandchildren are at school.

The Private Sector

Leisure is big business – the leisure industry in the UK employs 1.8 million people and accounted for somewhere in the region of £68 billion in 1989 (Benington and White, 1988, p. 2). Consumer expenditure on leisure between 1982 and 1988 grew in real terms by 27.3 per cent (Henry, 1993, p. 155). The industry is dominated by a small number of conglomerates whose interests span the worlds of television production, television rentals, betting shops, marinas, fast food chains, travel agencies, ten pin bowling alleys, leisure centres and theme parks. A typology of the private sector in leisure was produced by John Roberts: see figure 7.3.

The increasing amount of leisure time has meant that there are more opportunities for private firms to capitalize on the public need to be amused. The biggest item of consumer expenditure is alcohol. Vast sums are spent on alcohol each year by the British public – in 1984 it amounted to £314,416 billion while in 1989 the average family spent nearly £7 a week, £6.92, on alcohol consumed away from home. (Gratton and Taylor, 1987, p. 27; Central Statistical Office, 1992, table 10.27). Excessive drinking can lead to serious consequences both for the drinker and for others. The best known of these is the association between excessive alcohol consumption and death and injury on the roads but it is also estimated that eight million working days are lost each year because of absence related to alcohol (Department of Health, 1992, p. 58).

Television, alcohol, tobacco, sex and gambling are the five most popular ways of spending our leisure time (Roberts, 1978, p. 28), and the private sector is involved in all of these areas to a greater or lesser extent. Television has a substantial public input in the shape of the BBC but the provision of television sets, rentals and everything else in the industry is in the hands of the private sector with commercial television expanding its market share via satellite and cable. For alcohol, tobacco and gambling the provision is entirely in the private sector sphere with the role of the public sector being to regulate and inspect. As the best things in life are free the role of the private sector

Figure 7.3 A taxonomy of leisure activities provided (wholly or in part) by the commercial sector

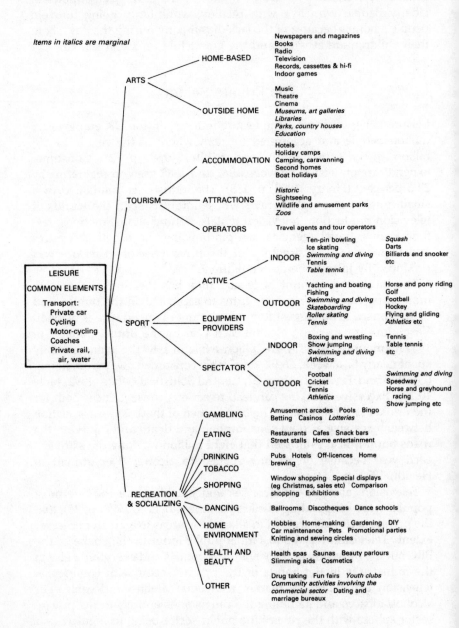

Source: John Roberts (1979), *The Commercial Sector in Leisure*, p. 44.

in sex is the most limited, although one should not ignore the 'sex industry': the pornographic magazine, film and book market, the thousands of prostitutes, and to a lesser extent the sex shops and companies who provide sex aids. This is all part of the 'commodification' of the leisure market (Benington and White, 1988).

Commodification has also entered the public sector, for museum directors and art galleries are encouraged to make money, to charge the public for admission and so forth. This has not affected all museums to the same extent and some national collections are still free but the fact remains that commercial principles have entered this world. The locations of the 'old' industries, which accounted for Britain being the first country in the world to industrialize, are now centres of historical interest. Bradford, for so long the world centre of the woollen and worsted industry, has successfully entered the tourist business and visitors go to the city to see what the 'dark, satanic mills' must have looked like. At the other end of the country, on the south coast, the Portsmouth naval dockyard has closed with the loss of many thousands of jobs and now the city markets itself as 'the flagship of maritime England', a naval heritage centre. Heritage is something that can be packaged and marketed and sold. There are plenty of examples of private firms who have started heritage museums and centres. The clearest statement of the Conservative government's commitment to the concept came in 1991 when they created the Department of National Heritage responsible for sport, arts and tourism.

Government and Leisure

It was during the Second World War that the state assumed some kind of responsibility for what might be called leisure when the government created the forerunner of the Arts Council, with its mission to bring the best of high culture to the population, taking it from the metropolitan elite. This was in tune with the democratic sensibility of wartime Britain, a mood which was sustained into the immediate post-war period after the Labour Party formed the government in 1945. The National Parks were established by the Access to the Countryside and National Parks Act of 1949 which designated a National Parks Commission to run them. The 1968 Countryside Act widened the responsibilities of the National Parks Commission giving it new responsibilities beyond its jurisdiction over the National Parks. The Countryside Commission, as it was now known, could help to finance the provision of countryside recreation through grants to local authorities. The new role was a response to the perceived social needs for recreation but also to growing environmental concerns about the dangers to the countryside (Henry, 1993, p. 21). This has become more marked in the 1980s because of the greatly increased dangers to the habitat posed by pressures for housing development and road construction. On some occasions these concerns, voiced by the Commission, have led it to oppose the plans of other parts of government. This may well be the reason why government decided to put its relationship with the Commission at arm's length by making it a quango in 1982 (Henry, 1993, p. 70).

The Sports Council was established by the Labour Government in 1965, in response to the perception that Britain was not doing as well at international sporting competitions because of the lack of central government leadership in sporting policy. At first the Sports Council was concerned with sporting excellence but then transferred its attention to improving participation in sports through the slogan 'Sport for All'. Over the years the Sports Council has been used as a conduit by successive governments to channel sums of money to combat delinquency, vandalism and ethnic divisions, and to meet the needs of disabled people.

In 1975 the Labour government issued a White Paper entitled *Sport and Recreation* which was to set the context for the development of central and local government policy on leisure for the next decade. The White Paper firmly placed the planning and policy for sport and recreation within the wider social services: 'The government accept that recreation should be regarded as "one of the community's everyday needs" and that provision for it is "part of the general fabric of the social services"' (Department of the Environment, 1975, para. 5). But there was a definite link with other areas of policy, chiefly that for young people. The White Paper commented: 'By reducing boredom and urban frustration, participation in active recreation contributes to the reduction of hooliganism and delinquency among young people' (para. 13). Since the publication of the White Paper government and local authorities have definitely promoted recreational activities in areas where frustration is most evident, namely, the inner cities. The White Paper claimed that 'recreational deprivation' was at its most acute in the inner cities, and in 1977 the Department of the Environment followed this up with a policy statement entitled *Recreation and Deprivation in Inner Urban Areas*. The government allowed sport and recreation schemes to be funded for the first time by the Urban Programme. The Sports Council, the government sponsored quango, has translated this policy into action through its 'Sport for All' campaign, aimed at increasing the participation of certain groups who traditionally have not involved themselves in sport. However, this special initiative did not attract the unemployed who persisted as a non-participant group (McIntosh and Charlton, 1985, p. 132).

Another target of the 'Sport for All' campaign was delinquency and crime. It was believed that extra spending on sport and recreation would lead to a decrease in crime figures. The Sports Council had some difficulty in persuading local authorities that sport was a cost-effective means of reducing crime, especially as their own evidence suggested that people from lower socio-economic groups within which the vandals were to be found, that is, the unskilled, were not coming along to the local authority Sports Centres. Sport and recreation were clearly responses to the inner city problem and this was demonstrated after the 1981 urban riots when the Sports Council allocated £3 million over three years for demonstration projects in areas of high social need. Doubts remain as to whether it was not just another palliative which did nothing to tackle the underlying problems in these areas of too few jobs, physical decay and loss of industry: indeed, it might be seen as redefining the urban problem as a leisure problem. Certain parts of the country have certainly benefited from this activity, mainly the inner cities. Nonetheless in the inner cities of Britain the problem of participation still exists. As Clarke and Critcher report, the skilled working class has gained from this policy of outreach but then so too has the professional middle class (1985, p. 153). A number of surveys have revealed, unsurprisingly, that low income households are infrequent users of Sports and Leisure Centres. By the mid-1980s only 7 per cent of the total number of local authorities in England and Wales had concessionary off-peak prices to encourage these groups (McIntosh and Charlton, 1985, p. 120). As we have seen, the fact that one has a low income is often linked to other factors which make participation more difficult, namely, lack of a car which is important for some sports where equipment needs to be transported, and insufficient income to be able to hire equipment regularly.

Local government is usually the means whereby funds for these projects are used to build the facilities. The local government system of England and Wales was reorganized in 1974 and many of the new authorities created Leisure Services or similarly titled departments which oversaw the running of the swimming baths, bowling greens, tennis courts, parks, recreation grounds and the many other forms of municipal provision for leisure. There was a big growth in the provision of facilities: in 1972 there were thirty local authority sports centres and less than 500 indoor swimming pools in England but six years later in 1978 there were 350 sports centres and more than 850 indoor pools (Sports Council, 1983, quoted in Henry, 1993, p. 22). Local authorities in the big urban areas understandably make the most extensive provision and the bulk of government funding for special social initiatives will go to these areas. Local authority departments have been affected by the move to compulsory competitive tendering as since 1989 local authorities have had to accept bids from the private sector for much of their leisure services work.

In the mixed economy of leisure the private sector plays a major part in the provision of sporting activities, all the way from the squash club to the Premier Division Football Club. Voluntary organizations dominate the provision of sport in so many ways as in each sport there is a voluntary organization which caters for members and organizes competition and events. In comparison, the local authority and the Sports Council are recent arrivals. Their role is to complement the role of the other two sectors for there is no sense in duplicating their work. The Sports Council has uncovered the groups who do not make sufficient use of the facilities provided by local authorities: the unemployed, women with small children, older people. As we have suggested, some of the reasons why these groups are infrequent users interact with the new patterns of inequality. If a Sports Centre is five miles away and the bus service is poor or non-existent then the non-car owner will not be using the squash courts there.

In the rest of this chapter we will examine the utilization of leisure facilities by two groups for whom local authorities have tried to improve take-up: women and the unemployed.

Women

Although women's leisure time has been increased by the decline in the number of children born, by the introduction of many household appliances which save time and labour and by increased life-expectancy, it is still the case that women have less leisure time, participate less in most leisure activities and draw on a narrower range of leisure activities than men. They also spend most of their leisure in and around home and family (Clarke and Critcher, 1985, p. 159).

Generally women's leisure is much less extensive than that of men. Because women have the major responsibility for the management of the home – child care and house cleaning and maintenance – this simply leaves them with less time to engage in leisure activities, whether this be the passive home-centred one of watching television or the more active pastimes such as participation in sport and socializing out of the house (see Deem, 1986, Green et al., 1990). Constraints on women's leisure are greater for working-class than middle-class women, who are more likely to have some sort of help in the home, child care and access to private transport. As there are fewer women than men holding driving licences this is a real constraint on women's independent leisure activity. Public transport can be very threatening for women, especially if they are on their own: the long waits at bus stops, the vulnerability to attack on buses and trains all make for fear of going out at night. In addition, there are problems for women with sexual harassment in pubs and clubs. Groups of women can be the victims of unwanted attention from other males who assume if there are no men with them that they are sexually available. This is even more the case if a woman goes into a pub on her own, as these are defined as male space. Green et al. in their study of 700 women in Sheffield found that married women were subject to quite a degree of control from their husbands over the kind of places they visited, and, indeed, over whether they visited a place at all. Although this is seen as the exercise of patriarchal control by Green et al. it could well have reflected their concern at the physical risks run by women out together. Several surveys have suggested that between 50 per cent and 70 per cent of women are frightened of going out after dark in cities (Atkins, 1990).

Women's leisure inside the home does display some different patterns to that of men. While men regard the home as a place of non-work, for very many women it is the site of work. This is obviously true of those women who do not go outside the home to engage in paid work but stay at home. These house managers find it very difficult to switch off from work, especially if they have children as even when they may be doing something for themselves they are still on call for them. For women with paid work outside the home then there does not seem to have been an appreciable increase in the amount of housework that their husbands do. On the whole these women are still expected to do the bulk of the household tasks, including the cooking and the care of the children, constituting what sociologists have called a 'double shift'.

Unemployed People

Sport and recreation is regarded as a way to help to combat the weakening of self-esteem and identity produced by unemployment. Unemployed people have been the target for a great number of local initiatives designed to increase their participation in sport and organized leisure provision. In the recent past, the schemes offered for unemployed people have taken three major forms: concessionary entrance to leisure centre activities, specific sessions for unemployed people and what is called 'social work in tracksuits' – helping people to identify their needs in sport and recreation (Glyptis, 1989, p. 147). Often a local authority will carry out all three of these activities.

Schemes for unemployed people cannot be divorced from those local authority projects aimed at disadvantaged communities where there is a low rate of participation in organized recreation. The government's Urban Programme has been used to finance, in whole or part, thousands of these initiatives. As well as reaching out to unemployed people they are intended to contact ethnic minorities, and especially women from ethnic minority communities. But there are wider aims than this which include the promotion of community identity, the creation of jobs and the use of derelict land (Pack and Glyptis, 1989, p. 1). Apart from the capital-intensive Sports Centres which have high running and staff costs there are many other smaller, but no less important, schemes such as the provision of kick about pitches for youngsters in urban areas, karting projects for youngsters or water sports on canals.

Despite the provision of sports schemes under the Urban Programme those areas with the highest unemployment did not have the greatest range or amount of provision for unemployed people. In the mid-1980s Northern Ireland had the highest unemployment rate in the UK but the second lowest rate of leisure provision for unemployed people (Glyptis, 1989, p. 145). It would appear that the political complexion of the local authority is the most important factor governing the provision of special facilities for unemployed people, whatever the level of unemployment. Labour authorities are much more likely to provide these facilities than Conservative controlled councils (p. 145).

Leisure as Social Policy

The identification with the rest of the social services promoted by central government and local authorities should give a clue as to how the public leisure sector might pursue its goals. There would seem to be a role here for an integration of policy objectives between different government departments. Clearly the Department of Health would have an interest in encouraging the promotion of those sports which will reduce the risk of heart disease and other costly conditions for the National Health Service. The fact that 48 per cent of adult males and 40 per cent of adult females are overweight indicates that there is a need for a change in the patterns of activity of the population (Activity and Health Research, 1992). Sports and leisure centres which encourage young people to engage in physically demanding sport have an important part to play because the evidence shows that for many these habits will be retained throughout life. Many leisure centres are now being used as part of a fitness programme in association with general practitioners, especially for older people.

The provision of more and more Sports Centres and sporting facilities would not be the only means to achieve an integrated policy. There would seem to be an excellent case for integrating transport, health and recreation policy to the extent that certain forms of mobility which are good for an individual's health are promoted. Walking is an excellent form of aerobic exercise, i.e. it promotes the action of the respiratory system. However, it is given the lowest priority by the Department of Transport and in some parts of our towns, cities and countryside it is very difficult to walk from one place to another because of the absence of safe pavements or obstructions from parked cars. Similarly cycling comes low on the list of priorities of the Department of Transport and the local authority highways departments in this country but is a very good form of exercise. Likewise, there would seem to be considerable sense in the Sports Council's strategy of targetting certain groups who are non-participants as this too should aid national fitness. Benington and White argue for an 'outreach' role for local authorities in which they would take it upon themselves to identify what the leisure needs of a local authority are and develop a leisure strategy for their area (1988).

The government has, through the Sports Council, attempted to encourage more people to take part in sporting activities but the message has been least successful with low income households. Many local authorities now provide concessionary entrance prices for people who are unemployed or are on low incomes yet this is not always what they want. One local authority which ran a free swimming session for unemployed people found that some of them were using the pool at other times, and having to pay, because they wanted to be with their friends rather than with other unemployed people (McIntosh and Charlton, 1985, p. 120; Audit Commission, 1990, p. 11).

Local authorities as the major channel of funds for sport and recreation from central government to the locality are subject to the pressures which they find in other areas of their work. It is noticeable how the provision of sport facilities and recreational opportunities for unemployed people and inner city dwellers improved after the riots of the early 1980s. Yet they were not the only group in 'leisure need'; for the claims of older people and disabled people were just as pressing. Local authorities are also prone to the political pressure of their electorate. It may well be that the electorate will welcome the building of a new leisure centre but this may not be the most socially advantageous scheme for a local authority area when balanced against the spending programmes of other departments. Even with the special efforts of local authority leisure staff it remains the case that the chief beneficiaries of leisure centres are white, male, mobile and mainly middle class. The question has to be asked: to what extent are local authorities providing a cheap version of facilities – squash courts, badminton, saunas – which this group could afford to buy at a private club?

Although local authorities and the Sports Council, acting on behalf of the government, are promoting the active participation in sport of as many people as possible it has to be remembered that the sponsorship of sport by commercial firms is now widespread. Two sectors of private industry have a particular interest in sponsoring sport: alcohol and cigarettes. Sponsorship of sporting events gives them a healthy image whilst at the same time promoting their product. This is particularly important to tobacco firms in the United Kingdom because they have been banned from advertising on television, although not in the press, for some years. By 1986 nearly 1,600 companies in the UK were sponsoring sporting events to the tune of around £129 million (Clark, 1989, p. 527). The sports chosen are ones which are known to be attractive to children – cricket, show-jumping, motor-racing – and the success of this sponsorship is revealed by the fact that children believe that there is cigarette advertising on television (Moss, 1992). The tobacco industry has been accused by the World Health Organization of causing a million premature deaths a year (Clark, 1989, p. 334). The Department of

Health estimates that 80 per cent of lung cancer is associated with smoking which means 26,000 deaths a year in England (Department of Health, 1992, p. 70). The Government's document on public health, *Health of the Nation*, estimates that 'among an average 1,000 young adults who smoke cigarettes regularly, about one will be murdered, about six will be killed on the roads, but about 250 will be killed before their time by tobacco' (p. 70).

Smoking and excessive alcohol consumption are two well known killers and entail the NHS in a great deal of expenditure every year. The lifestyle perspective now being adopted by some health authorities in their health promotion work is welcome but it is of course dwarfed by the anti-health propaganda of multinationals who wish to encourage a car-dependent way of life with high consumption of alcohol, cigarettes and unhealthy foods.

Leisure provision of the kind discussed here can certainly help an individual's self-esteem and physical fitness but it is doubtful whether it can supply the satisfactions, status and self-identity that paid work provides. Quite clearly the problem of unemployment will not be solved by the building of more and more leisure centres! Besides, in leisure, as in other aspects of social life, class, status and gender impinge on their consumption. The word is used advisedly because so much of leisure is, in fact, part of consumption. All the electronic products which appeal so much, the latest CD Rom and video games are part of a culture of consumption in which the market is the arbiter of what is fashionable. Nowhere does this seem to be more true than with children's computer games which proved an extremely lucrative market for 'entertainment corporations'. The status of consumption-related activities shows little sign of loosening its hold.

What should be the relationship between leisure and policy? A liberal perspective denies that it should be anything more than a residual one, that is to say, that the state should supply leisure provision where no one else – the voluntary sector or the commercial sector – has done so. To do more than this, it is argued, is to take on an impossibly open-ended commitment. This view rejects the claim that recreation is a part of citizenship and argues that the state should not attempt to meet leisure needs. It is far better to let the market allocate resources where there is a demand. The public's tastes and interests are so numerous and capable of such indefinite extension that the state cannot realistically undertake to satisfy them all (Roberts, 1978, p. 155).

In contrast, social democrats focus on the inequalities generated in the use of, and access to, leisure provision. Social democrats often believe that extended state involvement in leisure policy can help reduce inequalities. Whannel argues, for example, in relation to arts funding that the state should give the bulk of its funding to activities which have higher rates of participation among women and ethnic minorities. They see the growth of state – both central and local government – leisure policy as developing out of the gradual extension of citizenship rights. This position puts an emphasis on the right of individuals to participate in sport and recreation if they should wish to do so and a concomitant stress on the providers to establish what the leisure needs of the population are. The third position can be described as 'neo-marxist'. This is critical of leisure policy as it holds that it has not achieved its goal of achieving social integration, but on this analysis it could not but fail to do so because of the capitalist hegemony which is exercised in society. The market determines the distribution of leisure opportunities which means that the ideology is that of individual consumers rather than citizens (Clarke and Critcher, 1985). Nonetheless proponents of a marxist position argue for local authorities to grant-aid voluntary activities especially those of disadvantaged groups.

Social policy in the sphere of leisure seems likely to remain a small presence but because it enjoys the power of the state it has the ability to be very influential at certain times. The market remains the prime allocator of goods and services but the state must play a role as regulator. The state also has an important function, as we have seen, in the provision of sport and recreation services for disadvantaged groups and communities where the private sector's services are too expensive or non-existent. Similarly a country which is serious about improving the health of the population will be concerned to promote active forms of recreation and leisure and to ensure that these are available and accessible to all sections of society.

As we saw in the chapter on Travelling, the car is a passport to many opportunities denied those who have to rely on public transport. Leisure and recreation are a good example of this and the reduced use of leisure and recreational facilities by the lower socio-economic groups is, in part, the result of the lower levels of car ownership among them. In the 1970s Hillman and Whalley reported that half of sports trips were made by car (1977, p. 103). Overall their conclusion was that participation in sport was consistently higher in households with access to a car (p. 105). They argued that if the location of users of sports centres was examined then there was a relatively high number of people who lived within one mile and walked to the centres but this decreased dramatically over one mile.

Their view was that this was evidence of suppressed demand among people living at greater distances than one mile from the sports centre. Public transport was not found to be greatly used by sports centre attenders. With the significant exception of a number of big-city sports centres which are situated close to good public transport, sports centres tend not to be linked to the public transport network. To a certain extent this reflects the fact that sites which would be at the apex of the public transport system are costly to build while the outer sites are cheaper and have more room for large car parks. However, they tend not to have very many people within walking distance of them and the public transport links are poor (p. 67).

Access to the countryside is generally seen as a necessity for urban dwellers and here too the connection between social class and access can be seen. Over the last thirty years the public transport system in this country has deteriorated. This is of course a direct consequence of the greatly increased car ownership which as we saw in the chapter on Travelling led to the spiral of decline in bus services. Rail services were cut back by the Beeching Report of 1963 which, as a consequence of its implementation, meant the removal of many rural and semi-rural lines all over the country. This process has continued, with mobility opportunities for non-car owners further deteriorating. The trip out to the country cannot now be made because the bus or the train no longer runs. One of the intentions behind the creation of country parks on the fringes of urban areas was to make open space available to people without access to a car yet in a majority of cases people arrive by car. In contrast, for car owners access has greatly increased. The National Trust has seen its membership climb and climb because it is a favourite pastime for many to get in their car on a Sunday afternoon and visit a stately home. Yet ironically the aims of the founders of the Trust nearly a hundred years ago were to enable poor city dwellers to visit the countryside (see Darley, 1990).

The Countryside Commission recognizes that 'countryside recreation is socially selective, dominated by the higher-income groups, car-owners, the better educated, and those in higher-status white collar occupations' (Glyptis, 1989, p. 35). One quarter of the population never visit the countryside. These non-visitors are predominantly the unemployed, people on low incomes, older people and ethnic minorities. This recognition is a start but the major factor which prevents these groups from enjoying our countryside is the lack of access. The same pattern holds in relation to visits to stately homes and beauty spots (Reid, 1989, p. 389).

Leisure travel – the use of the car for recreational purposes in the countryside – coupled with the increasing trend towards population growth in rural areas made possible by the car threatens to make quiet, country lanes a thing of the past (Countryside Commission, 1992). Yet the bias towards the rural as the touchstone of authenticity – embodied in the Archers, Emmerdale Farm and countless stories of country life – shows no sign of diminishing with the result that large areas of countryside will see their roads become much more congested if Department of Transport traffic forecasts are correct.

In this chapter we have examined the leisure experience of only two groups in the population – women and unemployed people – and there are of course many other groups of people whose leisure needs and interests influence policy makers. One under-represented group in the world of leisure management are older people. By definition those who are retired have a great deal of leisure time but face difficulties in being able to enjoy it. Naturally one cannot generalize about older people for they are as disparate a group of people as the rest of the adult population, and one clear point which emerges is that their access to leisure activities is dependent upon their material prosperity. More older people are living to enjoy their retirement and a better standard of living for the majority of retired people is now possible. Specialist firms now cater for the holiday needs, housing needs and other needs of retired people yet of course there are still going to be two nations in old age, the rich and the poor, or more accurately for today, the poor and the rest of the population.

Most of the late twentieth-century descriptions of the future are about a society where leisure is much more widespread than it is now. This has been the goal of utopian thinkers for some centuries – a society where the need to labour in order to provide the subsistence necessary for the maintenance of life would be replaced by fewer hours devoted to work. Today in the poor world, which contains the majority of the world's population, this is still the case: if they do not work then they will not eat. But in the advanced industrial societies in the twentieth century such a surplus has been created that it is possible for most sections of the working population to enjoy some leisure. It needs to be borne in mind, however, how recent this phenomenon is for most people. Looked at from the viewpoint of sustainability then some forms of leisure are undesirable: the large out of town theme parks, however much fun they are, encourage the use of cars and people often drive considerable distances to reach them. Leisure is part of a culture of consumption. The major forms of leisure activity have not been discussed here but they include shopping as leisure – increasingly taking the form of a trip to an out of town shopping centre for a 'day out'. The booming market for electronic games among children is another manifestation of how the market is the arbiter as to what is fashionable. 'Entertainment corporations' are now able via their multi-media organization to create a world-wide market for certain of their products and to promote this through their control of certain media outlets.

Discussion Questions

1 Examine the arguments for and against charging for admission to museums and art galleries.
2 Should the state have a leisure policy?

Further Reading

Ian P Henry, *The Politics of Leisure Policy* (Macmillan, 1993) places the discussion of leisure in the context of political ideology and government structures. John Clarke and Chas Critcher, *The Devil Makes Work* (Macmillan, 1985) is a neo-marxist critique of leisure studies. Fred Coalter, with Jonathan Long and Brian Duffield, *Recreational Welfare: the rationale for public leisure policy* (Avebury, 1988) relates leisure to social policy.

References

Activity and Health Research (1992), *Allied Dunbar National Fitness Survey*, Allied Dunbar, Health Education Authority and the Sports Council.
Atkins, S (1990), 'Personal security as a transport issue', *Transport Reviews*, 10, 2, 111–25.
Audit Commission (1990), *Sport for Whom? Clarifying the Local Authority Role in Sport and Recreation*, London: HMSO.
Benington, J and White, J (1988), *The Future of Leisure Services*, Harlow: Longman.
Central Statistical Office (1992), *Social Trends*, 22, London: HMSO.
Cherry, G (1984), 'Leisure and the home: a review of changing relationships', *Leisure Studies*, 3, 35–52.
Clark, E (1989), *The Want Makers: Lifting the Lid off the World Advertising Industry: How They Make You Buy*, London: Coronet.
Clarke, J and Critcher, C (1985), *The Devil Makes Work: Leisure in Capitalist Britain*, London: Macmillan.

Coalter, F with Long, J and Duffield, B (1988), *Recreational Welfare: the Rationale for Public Leisure Policy*, Aldershot: Avebury.

Countryside Commission (1992), *Trends in Transport and the Countryside*, Manchester: Countryside Commission.

Darley, G (1990), *Octavia Hill*, London: Constable.

Deem, R (1984), *All Work and No Play?*, Milton Keynes: Open University Press.

Department of the Environment (1975), *Sport and Recreation*, Cmnd. 6200, London: HMSO, London.

Department of Health (1992), *The Health of the Nation: a Strategy for Health in England*, Cm 1986, London: HMSO.

Glyptis, S A (1989), *Leisure and Unemployment*, Milton Keynes: Open University Press.

Glyptis, S A and Chambers, D A (1982), 'No place like home', *Leisure Studies*, 1, 247–62.

Gratton, C and Taylor, P (1987), *Leisure in Britain*, Letchworth: Leisure Publications.

Green, E et al. (1990), *Women's Leisure, What Leisure?*, London: Macmillan.

Henry, Ian P (1993), *The Politics of Leisure Policy*, London: Macmillan.

Hillman, M and Whalley, A (1977), *Fair Play for All: a study of access to sport and informal recreation*, London: Political and Economic Planning.

McIntosh, P and Charlton, V (1985), *The Impact of Sport for All Policy 1966–1984*, London: Sports Council.

Moss, R (1992), 'Health and Television', *The Health Summary*, December.

Pack, C and Glyptis, S A (1989), *Developing Sport and Leisure: good practice in urban regeneration*, Department of the Environment, London: HMSO.

Reid, Ivan (1989), *Social Class Differences in Britain: Life-chances and Life-styles*, 3rd edn, London: Fontana Press.

Roberts, John (1979), *The Commercial Sector in Leisure*, London: Sports Council/ SSRC.

Roberts, Kenneth (1978), *Contemporary Society and the Growth of Leisure*, Longman.

Townsend, Peter (1979), *Poverty in the United Kingdom*, Harmondsworth: Penguin.

Urry, J (1990), *The Tourist Gaze: Leisure and Travel in Contemporary Societies*, London: Sage.

8

CONSUMERS OR CITIZENS?

Social life has changed dramatically in the last few decades prompted by the new technologies, by the new spatial distribution of industry, retailing and commerce, by the attempts to overcome inequalities based on gender, by changing family forms and by the collapse of work opportunities for a large section of the population. Social Policy cannot any more be limited to the five services which used to characterize the 'welfare state' – personal social services, health, education, social security and housing – without reference to the interconnections between these services and other areas of policy. The major changes described in this book have led to the generation of new forms of inequality which affect the welfare of individuals and their families: lack of mobility, inaccessibility, exclusion. As the economy and society have changed, those who are without the keys to participation – the access to the technology and goods – are denied many of the opportunities available to their fellow citizens. The growing privatization of social life has seemingly made the possession of consumer goods more important than ever before and yet we are conscious, as no previous generation has been, of the limits to material accumulation because of the environmental consequences of our systems of production and consumption. The title of this chapter encapsulates the two major contemporary views of the relationship between individuals and the state: as consumers of services or as citizens who use services. As the Conservatives have been in power since 1979 they have been able to shape and mould public services in order to fit their conceptions of what the role of the state should be, and their new approach to the organization and management of the state has had a considerable impact upon social and public policy.

Conservative governments since 1979 have subscribed to the view that there had been too much effort expended by the state in trying to reduce inequalities – by the provision of social services and the redistribution of wealth – with the result that entrepreneurs have been handicapped by the high tax burden; the consequence for this country was a failure to compete successfully with the leading economies of Western Europe. The government set out to change the thinking of the British people, to encourage the growth of an 'enterprise culture' in which a 'can do' philosophy would prevail. Business, commerce, trade and industry, these were the keys to our revival as an economy and as a society. The Thatcher government criticized those post-war Conservative governments who, like Labour governments, had pushed the boundaries of the welfare state wider and wider. The welfare state was one of the reasons why Britain was uncompetitive on the world economic market.

The Conservative governments believed that the state had to be taken out of people's lives and this meant lowering taxes, principally income tax, but also reducing the range of state activities. It was for this reason that the 'right to buy' was introduced for all council tenants in 1980 and recalcitrant councils who wanted to keep their housing stock were forced to sell it off to those tenants who wished to purchase their own homes. The state had to be removed from certain areas of life: the Thatcher government dismantled parts of the machinery which had enabled the post-war state to grow.

Privatization was the key policy – in effect denationalization – and this had the advantage of spreading the values of the enterprise culture as the public were encouraged to buy shares in the newly privatized companies. The aim was to make capitalism popular, to make people feel that they too were part of the share-owning society, just as earlier they had become homeowners and car owners, which the Conservatives felt gave them a stake in the society. The privatization programme of the Conservative governments may be said to have started with the sale of the public telecommunications monopoly British Telecom in 1984. It proceeded with the sale of the state airline, British Airways, and then the public utilities of electricity, gas and water.

The concept of privatization denotes the change from public to private enterprise: nationalized industries were denationalized. Henceforward companies are listed on the Stock Exchange and act as any private company would do, although they are generally very large concerns. The rationale behind this massive sale of state assets was that once freed from government control the organizations would be free to determine and pursue their own goals, thus leading to greater efficiency and hence profitability. Behind the government's sale of shares in the public sector organizations was a strong conviction that its role was not to make decisions about goods and services. As the Chancellor of the Exchequer, Nigel Lawson, remarked: 'the business of government is not the government of business' (Dunn and Smith, 1990, p. 37). The market was to be the allocator of rewards and penalties for successful and unsuccessful firms and it was into this market that the newly privatized institutions were sent. Privatisation, although a hotly contested political issue in the UK, has proved a very attractive policy with foreign governments throughout the globe.

Deregulation – the abolition of bars on competition in the public sector – has been the other principal method whereby government has changed the organization of the public sector in the 1980s. Restrictive legislation which permitted only the state or its nominees to provide a service has been swept away. The intention has been to encourage the private sector to compete with public agencies and in the process raise the standards and quality of service to the customer. Local authority activity has been greatly affected by this policy. In 1980 the government introduced legislation to enable local authorities, if they so wished, to put contracts out to tender. The 1988 Local Government Act stipulated that a wide range of local authority activities must be contracted out. On many occasions this has meant that the authority's own workforce has not won the contract and as a result there have been redundancies. This has not been an important concern for central government which has viewed the deregulation process as a means of ensuring greater economy as well as efficiency in the public sector. This retreat by the state from important areas of national and local life has meant that it is no longer the obvious agency for the delivery of services: there are clear examples of this process at work in the personal social services where the NHS and Community Care Act 1990 has expanded the opportunities for private market provision.

Prior to the restructuring of governmental activity the New Right had promoted a powerful case against institutional arrangements which met need, pre-eminently the welfare state services. Broadly two schools of thought can be distinguished: the New Right which tends to rely on an economic analysis of the corrosive effect of state welfare on the working of the economy; furthermore, the New Right believes that state welfare damages the initiative and enterprise of ordinary people. Its remedy for the sickness of both the economy and the individual is the market. Alongside this is the neo-conservative school of thought which places great emphasis on the importance of traditional arrangements in social life – the nuclear family, the work ethic, the church, respect for law and order – and tends to see social problems as related to the decline of these values.

The state has to change its mode of operation in the future in order to relate to the diversity which our society now exhibits. In some part this is already occurring. Local authorities have not only had to respond to the *diktats* of Conservative governments who have insisted that they introduce contracting out, privatization and deregulation, but also have themselves responded to what they saw as the deficiencies of the old-style municipalities: remoteness from the electorate, control by a small number of politicians, policy determination by a professional elite without public participation. Many Labour and Liberal local authorities have accepted some part of the New Right's case against local government in that they acknowledge that they have not always been in touch with the wishes of the electorate. A variety of initiatives have been introduced by councils to rectify this (Gyford, 1991). The chief remedy has been the Public Service Orientation – which promotes decentralization with the aim of getting closer to the public so that the local authority no longer appears so remote because one can pay one's rent or enquire about a bus-pass in a neighbourhood office, within walking distance. It also involves local government adopting the techniques of private sector firms who wish to establish what the public think of their product – they hire market researchers to ascertain what the public make of the local authority (Stewart, 1992).

The 'Citizen's Charter' initiative of the Major government, launched in 1991, has been an attempt to raise the quality of services by specifying exactly what users of the public sector can expect from the organization and then introducing compensation when these standards are not met. It represents a commitment to the public sector and in that sense it is a move away from Mrs Thatcher's view of the public sector as a set of services which encouraged dependency in the population. But the Charters are for consumers rather than citizens. The Citizen's Charter seeks to mimic the market through its emphasis on competition, privatization and contracting out. It is a model of citizenship as consumerism. The government believes that no charter is necessary in the private sector because the customers can take their money elsewhere. Moreover the private sector provides models of quality which can be incorporated into the public sector.

The Citizen's Charter initiative of the Conservative government outlines a standard of service which we can expect to receive from the public sector. If this is not complied with then the user of the service can receive an apology and in some cases compensation. The Charter stipulates that the public sector provide full and comprehensive information about their services. This has led to the publication of exam results for individual schools throughout the country and data on the punctuality of trains by British Rail, to quote but two outcomes. Subsequently the government has published a range of charters which include the Patient's Charter for the NHS, a Parent's Charter for schools and Charters for Further and Higher Education. At the same time that it announced the Citizen's Charter the government declared that it was to proceed with a major piece of privatization – the ending of the British Rail monopoly on running trains. The Charter contains a commitment to the public sector but within the context of a continuation of the Thatcherite policies of de-regulation and privatization.

Consumerism

Since the 1950s we have witnessed the growth of the consumer market. This process, the equipping of homes with consumer durables, is much more than this. For when we use the term consumerism, we are literally speaking of an ideology, an 'ism', which has a power as great as that of other ideologies such as socialism or liberalism. This is not always clear for we have no Consumer Party, no consumerist newspapers or radio stations proclaiming the values of the consumerist way of life. But look again. It might be said that all the major political parties in the UK do precisely that. Both Labour and Conservative Parties accept the primacy of consumption and would not threaten their electoral position by proposing policies which ran in the face of consumerism. For example, there is an excellent environmental case for limiting the production of cars but this is accepted to be electoral suicide for any major political party. Similarly we have a mass media which is largely sustained by advertising – the advertising of consumer goods – so that in a way we can say that consumerism is a powerful ideology precisely because it is taken for granted, it is the common sense of our age and all the more powerful for that.

There is another more subtle sense in which consumerism is important for understanding our time. Not only is it pervasive as a way of life in Western societies but it also seems to have entered into the psyche of many people in Western societies so that they see themselves as consumers, they achieve their identity through the process of consumption and thus have a deep attachment to the kind of society in which we live. This process, the creating of identity by the individual – it is literally possible to shop around for an identity – takes the place of older forms of identity which people inherited – from their family, their social location, their class. The extent to which consumerism has become embedded in our society and in the consciousness of individuals is open to question and will become apparent in the remainder of this century if the imperatives of ecology and sustainability are to be taken seriously, if limits are set – apart from those of the market – on the extent to which individuals can consume.

There is a plurality of choice open to individuals in the modern world. We have seen how mobility means that people can leave a certain location quite easily which is an option not available to their forebears. Modern social life is much more segmented than in the past, the connections between leisure and work and community are no longer as close and binding as they once were in traditional societies.

Home

In contemporary society there has been a marked preference towards the home by individuals. The era of public events is not over – clearly people still go out to concerts, theatre and countless other forms of amusement and diversion – but it is on the wane. It is being replaced by a lifestyle in which the home is much more important for an individual's sense of self.

Home plays a key symbolic role in modern society as a place of comfort and recreation. Social life increasingly revolves around the home. Information Technology has increased the value of the home as a place for work and for electronic leisure. Car ownership means that many of us have much greater choice as to where to locate our homes. Broadcasting technology means that the home, via the medium of the satellite and the television, can be in touch with developments all over the globe: so we have the phenomenon of the globalization of the media but its reception being centred on the most private part of a person's life, the home. Home is also the place where gender relations are reproduced and reinforced: because of the division of space between family members, the kitchen is generally regarded as a female area while the garden is seen as the preserve of the male. The home is also the place where we display the consumer goods which we have acquired. It is, if you like, a show-case for the audio equipment or fine furniture. The home is often the site where we can be ourselves, and we can also express ourselves through the furnishings which we purchase or the decorative styles we adopt. As we saw in the chapter on shopping, consumption is a form of lifestyle defined as a set of practices which enable us to articulate our self-identity as well as fulfil a particular set of needs (Giddens, 1991, p. 81). The home is the place in which the social relations of consumption are negotiated.

One of the paradoxes of modern social life is the way in which homes are integrated into world-wide systems of communication via television technology but are much more isolated one from another. We have reviewed the reasons for this – the greater number of people in paid employment, the use of private cars which means there are far fewer people walking along the pavements of our cities and towns – but it has consequences for many sections of our population: children who cannot play on the street, elderly people who suffer more from social isolation just because there are not the number of people around that there used to be when they were younger, women who find the streets a place of great hazard because of the paucity of pedestrians. As the home has become more of a safe haven then the street has become for some a site of fear.

Sustainability

Consumer societies were warned of the possible outcome of their year-by-year burgeoning use of resources in pursuit of ever higher standards of living with the publication of *Limits to Growth* in 1972 (Meadows et al., 1972). It warned that the world did not have sufficient resources – of oil, of minerals, of food and other necessities – to be able to allow Western industrial consumer societies to continue to pursue economic growth. At some point in the future, a halt would have to be called to the process of year on year growth, as shortages of basic materials would arise. Since that time, the environmental crisis has become much more pressing as certain major malfunctions in the carrying capacity of the planet have emerged –

notably the greenhouse effect and the holes in the ozone layer – which have forced some environmental measures onto the agenda of the world's political leaders, the banning of CFC and the need to reduce the production of greenhouse gases in particular.

Sustainability was first put on the agenda by *Limits to Growth* and in the 1980s became the dominant concept in discussions of the environment. It means, to use Jacobs's definition:

> the environment should be protected in such a condition and to such a degree that environmental capacities (the ability of the earth to perform its various functions) are maintained over time, at least at levels sufficient to avoid future catastrophe, and at most at levels which give future generations the opportunity to enjoy an equal measure of environmental consumption. (Jacobs, 1991, pp. 79–80)

The concept puts the needs of future generations at the heart of the environmental argument, although one can argue about the way in which the 'environmental capacities' are maintained through time. A particular objection would be that population growth will demand a constantly increasing growth in wealth in order to sustain present levels, otherwise one is handing on a diminished stock. The extent to which the consumer society is compatible with sustainability is doubtful. Of late, the immediate response of many sections of industry, commerce and retailing has been to move towards 'greening': stressing the green nature of their products or their industry. But there is an extent to which this is only done in response to consumer feedback. 'Green consumerism' is an advance but it has obvious limitations for sometimes the cost of the greenest product will be beyond the reach of the poor (Irvine, 1989, p. 17). A fundamental challenge to the consumer society comes from countless Greens who argue that a consumerism which stimulates artificial wants is inherently damaging for the environment as it is promoting a society predicated on economic growth in order to satisfy these demands. This is a radical political perspective in that it entails a reduction in the aspirations of consumers and an abandonment of the ceaseless striving for goods. Poverty itself is not sustainable as it is directly counter to equity which is implied by the definition of sustainability.

This brief outline of the green position is enough to show how divergent this thinking is from the dominant ideologies of Western societies. Implicitly or explicitly both major parties in the UK have accepted the premisses of a consumer society and would be unwilling to challenge them as they fear it would mean electoral defeat. Nonetheless there would seem to be a role for ecological considerations – in the example of energy taxation, for instance. But there is another side to the sustainability argument and this is the fact that most of the world's population do not enjoy the standard of living that we enjoy in the Western world or anything like it. The question then becomes the extent to which it is permissible to continue to enjoy this life-style when it is denied to the majority of the people of the world and in fact is only possible because of the poor trade conditions that they receive from the rich countries. Communications technology has ensured that the plight of starving Africans can be beamed around the world and that Africans with television sets can see the standard of living that the Western world enjoys. Green thought has permeated most political ideologies and social movements. There are green capitalists as well as eco-feminists. There is a great variety of thinking about how environmental considerations can impact on different areas of activity.

Given that there have to be changes in the form and nature of the economy and society in order to incorporate environmental considerations the implementation of green measures is still fraught with difficulties, especially along the Social Policy dimension. The role of government in relation to the various sectors of social life which we have reviewed in this book is as regulator, inspector, legislator. All of these roles are required in relation to environmental policy but they entail some hard thinking about the distributional consequences. Jacobs points out that environmental taxation should not fall disproportionately on the poor. If this were to be the case then it could, quite properly, be criticized as socially regressive. Jacobs cites the example of energy taxes where an increase in the price of gas, electricity and oil would fall disproportionately on the poor whose energy consumption is half that of high income households. For some groups among the poor a cut in fuel consumption could have severe consequences, particularly for old people at risk of hypothermia and for small babies. Jacobs proposes that social benefits be increased in order to take into account the general rise in the cost of energy. The difficulty with this recommendation is that there is no way that the government can control the extent to which this extra money will be used to pay for fuel bills. This is more than the point that the poor may go and spend the money on other goods and services, but really that the government cannot control what the general movement of prices and wages in the economy will be which might force low-income consumers to use their increased benefits to purchase other services. An alternative would be some kind of means testing whereby help was given with fuel bills by the government. But as Jacobs points out, recent work shows that the bills of the poor are large ones because they do not have the capital to invest in proper insulation and other energy-saving measures (1991, p. 176).

Fiscal measures of this kind, although not yet on the immediate political agenda, are not too far-fetched for contemporary political discourse. But at the centre of the green argument is a belief that the life-styles of the West are unsustainable and as a consequence certain wants which the population currently has should be reduced or, in the long term, eliminated. A distinction is made between wants and needs with many of the consumer durables of western societies being categorized as wants rather than needs. They argue that psychological data seem to suggest that the main determinants of happiness are not related to consumption but more to family, marriage, satisfaction with work, leisure. Easterlin showed that the reported differences in happiness between countries from the rich world and the poor world were small despite the big differences in income levels between those countries (1974). In America the 'very happy' section of the population has been around one third since the 1950s, despite the big increase in material prosperity in that country (Durning, 1992, p. 39). The Worldwatch Institute has divided the population of the world into the following consumer classes (p. 27):

World Consumption Classes, 1992

Category of Consumption	Consumers (1.1 billion)	Middle (3.3 billion)	Poor (1.1 billion)
Diet	meat, packaged food, soft drinks	grain, clean water	insufficient grain, unsafe water
Transport	private cars	bicycles, buses	walking
Materials	throwaways	durables	local biomass

Green thought is in some fundamental ways incompatible with consumerism and has more obvious affinities with citizenship. The Green ethic would claim that citizenship has to embrace ethical consideration of the harm that any individual can cause the planet. It enjoins upon citizens a wider loyalty than that to their country – to the planet as a whole. In that sense, then, the Greens would stress the responsibility side of the citizenship equation.

Citizenship

The 1980s saw the idea of the market as resurgent all over the world but particularly in the UK where the Conservative government has extolled its virtues to the nation and, as we have seen, encouraged the public sector to follow the management models of the private sector. The centre and Left in British politics have been searching for a 'big idea' with which to counter the appeal of the market and many think that they have found it in the concept of Citizenship. Citizenship can perhaps provide a clue as to how the forms of exclusion which we have surveyed in this book could be reduced in their impact.

The dominant conception of citizenship within Social Policy and Administration is that articulated by T H Marshall in 1949 shortly after the creation of the welfare state in Britain. Marshall (1963) argued that the development of modern British society had seen the emergence of three kinds of rights: civil, political and social. Civil rights are those which are to do with the legal status of individuals and their relationship with the state, for instance the right to habeas corpus and trial by jury; political rights are the right to vote, and by social rights Marshall meant the right to social security and other welfare provision which the welfare state had created. In the 1980s social citizenship was resurrected as a defence of the welfare state. In the context of this book it is worth taking a look at Marshall's original formulation of the term social citizenship:

> By the social element I mean the whole range from the right to a modicum of economic welfare and security to the right to share to the full in the social heritage and to live the life of a civilised being according to the standards prevailing in society. (Marshall, 1963, p. 74)

Subsequently with the emergence of welfare bureaucracies the discussion of social citizenship has been almost entirely around the role of the state in the protection of social rights. It is doubtful if this was ever adequate as a consideration of the relationship between welfare and the individual but it can no longer be seen in this way given the rise of the consumer society and the reduced role of the state as a welfare agency. Consumerism, privatization of everyday life, home-centredness all point to the importance of other sectors of social life for the welfare of individuals in contemporary society. This is not to say that the state does not have an involvement in these areas: food, the environment and transport are among some of the areas of life in which the state plays a role. The nature of that role obviously varies from sector to sector but largely consists in the planning and regulation of sectors and the inspection of goods and services.

A social citizenship perspective on the areas of social life discussed in this book would posit the view that the state's role is to intervene in these areas in order to protect the rights and aspirations of citizens. This could take a great variety of forms. In relation to shopping it would mean that local authorities would have much greater powers to stop out-of-town retail developments which threatened the integrity of city centres. Where these were in operation it would mean the provision of bus services to ensure that low income shoppers could reach these stores. Going beyond this it might be the subsidy, through reduction in council tax, of small shops in the community in recognition of the importance which these small businesses play in the sense of neighbourliness and social contact in communities. In the world of Information Technology it could take the form of providing a late twentieth-century version of the public library, but this library would consist of computers and software which would enable citizens to access material only otherwise available to private firms or individuals. Universal access to communications and information facilities would mean that people could use the information which they obtain to make sense of their rights in other areas of their life. Disabled people could make far more extensive use of the Information Technology equipment available to them if finance was available for its utilization.

One could imagine that the extension of citizenship in this manner would require a Citizen's Charter of a very different kind to that launched by the government in 1991. It might include the right to travel, which would entail a reversal of present policies with a boost to public transport which would extend the abilities of poor and disabled people to reach their destinations. A collective form of transport such as buses or trains would give greater opportunities to low income people to travel as would concessions to various groups such as pensioners or the unemployed.

Much less emphasis in recent years has been placed on the responsibilities, duties or obligations which stem from citizenship. If citizenship is to have meaning then it has to include duties which the citizen owes to the wider society, to his or her family and friends. These might be said to include the payment of taxes, and respect for the rule of law. Parents may be said to have duties to see that their children are properly socialized and do not engage in anti-social behaviour. This ethic of responsibility is most clearly seen in arguments about the environment. Environmental policies presume a certain level of cooperation from citizens in making them work. This ethic also presumes that firms will live up to their environmental responsibilities and not endanger the local population or the environment by their actions.

This ethic is difficult to put into practice because it is in direct contrast to the consumerist ethos of modern society. It is much easier to persuade people to spend money and take home their packaging rather than to persuade them to bring their used bottles and cans to the supermarket's recycling centre on their next visit. The tradition of citizenship dating back to Ancient Greece involves active participation by individuals in the society's institutions. It is through this participation that they acquire citizenship (Oldfield, 1990, chapter 8).

Citizenship cannot become the 'big idea' for Social Policy without acknowledging the changes in the locality which have occurred since 1945. We need to remember the oldest meaning of the term, that is, the status of inhabitant of a town or city. Many of the inequalities of contemporary life are to do with place: supermarkets closing, poor transport, inaccessible facilities, dangerous streets. To the extent that citizenship implies a loyalty or obligations to a place then it can be seen that the term has been seriously eroded. Underlying these conceptions is the issue of access. In transport, Information Technology, to a certain extent in broadcasting and in shopping and leisure as well access has become very important. Its importance stems from the fact that our modern system of technologies, whilst it has greatly improved the speed at which information can be transmitted and the speed with which individuals with cars can reach certain locations, with all sorts of consequences for the location of industry and homes, has actually led to a deterioration in the access of certain groups in the population. Clearly accessibility takes a number of forms. Access to certain forms of information technology requires a certain knowledge of computer systems or software. In transport the usual usage is in relation to geographical location. Physical accessibility refers to the ease with which people can reach certain places and the ease with which they can reach destinations at which they can carry out certain activities (Moseley, 1979, p. 57).

The role of the state in the promotion of accessibility is crucial for it cannot be expected that the private sector will have the inclination, or indeed the ability, to do anything about this problem. Accessibility is of course a particular problem for different parts of the country, being a particularly important issue for the car-less in rural areas where the absence of a car does not only impair one's ability to shop, reach health facilities and so forth but also affects the quality of one's life as places of entertainment cannot be reached without access to a car. The role of the state might be said to facilitate access for the car-less but this would involve a reversal of present government policies for the transport sector where the move to deregulation has meant a cut in the number of services provided.

In this mobile society the discourse of citizenship becomes much more problematical for the fixity of place, of neighbourhood, of community is no longer available to give us a sense of self. Instead that sense of self is engendered through the consumption of products and the universally acceptable means of exchange, money. Yet there is a strong sense in which the intervention of the state in everyday life since the nineteenth century and the growing mass of laws concerning the education, health and welfare of the people imply citizenship: both duties and rights. As Roche has demonstrated the state has duties towards its children, to educate them to take a part in the society, a duty which it can be said to be failing to fulfil, if as in Britain, so many children leave school without qualifications or skills. Similarly families might be said to have duties towards their children to instil in them the belief that they should work to make use of the opportunities which are presented to them. Roche makes the point in relation to Information Technology, where unless the state educates its children in its uses then in some important sense the nation will not be equipped to compete with other leading industrial workforces in the next century (Roche, 1992, p. 235). But for young people themselves the new technology can make exclusion worse: if they do not have access to computers and have not learnt the necessary skills then they can be excluded from society by virtue of the fact that they are 'information-poor'.

In the areas of social life documented in this book it is difficult to see how a concern to safeguard the position of those who suffer from the inequalities generated by the market can be protected without recourse to the state in some form or another. The state as regulator has become a much more important function, both for central and local government, and the clue to its new role might well be found in this concept. Public services clearly need to be rescued from the tarnished, under-funded image they have acquired in the UK and which they do not possess in other Western European countries.

Social life is not something that can easily be altered by the actions of the state. The reasons why we shop and travel and work and all the other activities of daily life are not determined by government policy. They can be affected by it but there are other powerful forces which bear upon the way we shop, travel, view and communicate. Obviously the organization of the economy is paramount, which in a modern economy includes the multifarious means by which sellers attempt to influence buyers: public relations, marketing, advertising. The certainties of class divisions appear to have disappeared so that we cannot (if we ever could) speak of class views of the world any longer. Instead these have been replaced by status groups of various kinds. There are numerous examples of these which tend to be based on the attitudes and aspirations of the people concerned towards the market. Fragmentation of life style has occurred in the last quarter of a century. There was much talk in the inter-war period of the 'masses' and 'mass culture' and 'mass taste' but in our own time this has been replaced by a diversity of styles, tastes and markets. The difficulties this has posed for manufacturers, and those who attempt to cater for this market have been immense, for the old certainties that men of a middle age in the working class will watch this television programme or like that sport or prefer that cigarette have broken down.

Many of the new freedoms – of mobility, of lifestyle, of consumption – have become possible by the widespread introduction of Information Technology and indeed technology itself. Technology in the widest sense is in part responsible for the changing work patterns: the ways in which industries are restructuring with a consequent need for many fewer workers, and those they do employ able in some cases to work from home or to have a much greater degree of flexibility than they enjoyed in the past.

To some extent consumerism has replaced citizenship as a source of identity and private satisfaction. Yet it might be said to be an ersatz form of identity. The institutions which used to provided an identity for citizens do not feel able to do so anymore: schools, colleges, churches, voluntary organizations have all suffered a loss of confidence in their ability to promulgate identity. As Lunt and Livingstone observe: 'The problem for the individual is to construct an authentic sense of identity in an unsupportive context' (1992, p. 170). Those who advocate social citizenship as an integrating concept for social policy have to consider whether it is possible to recreate a supportive context, a public realm. Marquand has provided a convincing account of the post-war dissolution of the public realm in Britain. He identifies reductionist individualism as the ideology which has seriously weakened the community and polity:

We collaborate with our fellows, not only because we have been ordered to or because we calculate that it is in our interests to, but because we have learned to, because we believe it is our duty to, because the ties of mutual obligation which derive from membership of a community impel us to. (Marquand, 1991, p. 218)

He believes that politics must become mutual education in which these ideas could be fostered. It would mean the reinvigoration of local government by extending many more powers to it.

New Inequalities

As well as the new policies on the role of the government in the economy, economic and social change have accelerated in the past decade. Old certainties built around certain enduring features have declined. In the working class the big battalions of labour, those who worked in the shipbuilding and mining industries, have suffered wholesale job losses. Unemployment has been the most divisive consequence of the restructuring of the economy. The spectre of mass unemployment returned and it now looks as though it will be a permanent feature of our economy and society. One of the key themes of this book has been the increasing importance of the home and the privatization of everyday life. Nowhere is this more apparent than in the realm of leisure where home-based activities are the preponderant forms of leisure in the late twentieth century. The increasing inequality is real enough with the 'pay per' television viewing which is emerging in our homes. The inequalities of leisure are also related to the sexual division of labour which reveal that many women have a lot less leisure than men. This is particularly so for the working-class woman.

These big changes in our economic and social life – the privatization of everyday life, the restructuring of the economy, the stress on individual identity – have drained collectivism of its meaning and strength.

It has been argued here that for many people the areas of social life we have examined are extremely important for their own sense of well-being and welfare. The welfare state was an attempt on one level to redress the inequalities of a capitalist society, although as we now know it was not very successful in that aim (see Le Grand, 1982). What is becoming clearer is that new inequalities have emerged since the 1940s which need to be taken into account when discussing the aims of social policy. Access has been highlighted as an area which impinges upon much of social life and on welfare state services. It demonstrates the inadequacies of the market in a stark manner for as the mobility of car-less people in the last thirty years has declined we have seen big advances in motorway construction, high speed trains, jet travel and transport expenditure in general. The debate on transport which has ignored the needs of the car-less shows the extent to which policy debate is structured around the needs of the adult population, ignoring the legitimate claims of children to be able to play in safety outside their homes or to travel short distances by themselves. One of the indices used to assess an old person's ability to look after themselves is shopping. Yet in many towns and cities the capacity to shop for oneself is being taken away from older people, not because they cannot walk but because shops are closing down as out-of-town provision mushrooms. Society can create disabilities: it is doing so by the general adoption of Information Technology which makes it more difficult for old people to check prices once they are at the store. There is already a widening gap between those with easy access to information and those who lack the computer hardware and knowledge to be able to tap into data sources. Access is important in the world of work – Pahl has remarked on the existence of 'work-rich' households where the contacts enjoyed by the household, often through the full-time worker, lead to more work (Pahl, 1984).

The policy areas we have described are almost entirely part of the private sector: shopping, information technology, broadcasting, leisure, work and travel are all dominated by the private sector and in the last decade there has been a diminution of state involvement through the process of privatization of existing state activity. The result has been a widening of inequality between the two thirds who are in work and participate in house and car ownership and the one third who do not have these advantages. What is at issue here is the implicit contract between state and the individual. What is the nature of the implicit deal which is struck between the citizen and the state? Since 1979 we have had Conservative governments who see the role of the state as supporting the market and are mistrustful of any attempt to use the state to redress inequalities. This has led to a run down in public provision and the promotion of the 'private is best' philosophy – although survey evidence shows that there was a continuing high level of support among the UK population for state provision in the 1980s, especially in the spheres of education and the NHS (Taylor Gooby, 1991, p. 125).

So far from a diminution of the role of the state the evidence presented here would suggest that any government interested in removing the new social inequalities would need to intervene more than has been done in the past. Naturally this would not involve a return to organizational models of state intervention favoured in the past like nationalization, but a state that was able to inspect and to regulate and to supply the deficiencies of the private sector. This would mean in some policy areas giving greater powers to local authorities to control developments of which they did not approve or to subsidize a state service, as in transport, which could not be provided by a private company. Having said this the internationaliz-ation of capital does mean that control by central or local government is not as straightforward as it used to be. The processes we have described – privatization, deregulation, contracting out – lead to a much greater fragmentation than there has ever been before. A state which wants to intervene in order to reduce inequalities now has a much more difficult task because decision making has become widely dispersed with many more layers of control and competing interests.

One of the most powerful ideas informing the dominant tradition in Social Policy and Administration until the 1970s was the notion that social policy was concerned to produce social integration. The chief exponent of this viewpoint was Richard Titmuss, who saw the National Health Service as the exemplar of a social institution whose values of universality and non-discrimination would lead to the growth of altruistic values within society. Over the last twenty years the small steps to produce greater social integration have been reversed by a considerable redistribution of wealth to the rich from the rest of society. Tax rates have been cut and various fiscal measures directed at the rich have been dispensed with. The Thatcher government was especially concerned to produce in this country an 'enterprise culture' in which entrepreneurial values of hard work, ambition and self-interest would be fostered. Quite apart from the advisability of attempting to steer Britain in this direction, it remained an agenda which was clearly never going to include the poorest in our society and disabled people and others who for reasons of age, poverty or location could not participate in the enterprise culture.

This book shows how processes of exclusion are at work within our society. A large number of people do not participate in the car-owning and property-owning democracy because they lack the wherewithal to buy themselves into this culture. A smaller number cannot participate because society is organized for the needs of sighted, ambulant people. Participation is a concept which has in the main been applied to the world of politics but as so much evidence shows this world is not really an influence in most people's lives, except possibly for the few weeks immediately prior to a general election. If poor people wanted to participate in politics then they would find that the costs are high: not just the membership fee of a party but the social life which accompanies active membership and is an essential part of political activism (Ward, in Golding, 1986).

Instead social life matters much more. The critical age in a teenager's life is not eighteen when he or she can vote but seventeen when they are allowed to drive a car. Late Victorians thought that it was a serious penalty to deprive somebody of the franchise but today a lifetime ban on driving a car would be viewed by most people as much more serious. Driving has achieved this high status because it is a passport to participation in any number of facilities, sports, entertainments and activities. To be car-less is to be excluded. One can hazard that a similar process may operate in the future in respect of computers where the 'information-rich' middle class will be able to tap into various data bases and electronic networks and thereby participate in the world in a way which will be denied to the 'information-poor' without computers. How this can be remedied is not easy to see. Consumerism is a way of seeing the world which allows no thought for those without money: by definition they do not participate. The extent to which this has happened in Britain in the 1980s was seen in the riots in various outer council estates and the evidence emerging about the lack of hope which pervades the minds of so many unemployed young people. The rise in crime has been associated with this. The 'underclass' is usually described as being people sited in a particular part of a city or on a particular estate. But the forms of exclusion which we have reviewed here do not of course only discriminate against a geographically identified underclass for they prevent disabled people, older people and others from full participation in the society. Peter Townsend's work has pointed to the significance of income for participation in our society (1979). A relative definition of poverty is an acknowledgement that poverty can consist in the deprivation or the exclusion from certain facilities in our society. Those excluded can suffer disadvantage in leisure, transport, sport and shopping as well as housing, health and education. Traditionally Social Policy has placed considerable emphasis on services but in the new world of the post-welfare state there is less opportunity to do this: the NHS and Community Care reforms have destabilized the work of health and local authorities as they are no longer able to think of themselves as providers of services.

Globalization – and particularly the spread of the mass media – has meant that it is much easier than ever before for the poor world to see what the rich world wears, eats and thinks. This has ensured that millions in the poor world now want to imitate these consumerist lifestyles. But it is consumer societies which inflict the maximum damage on the world's environment.

We have looked at the way in which inequalities affect the lives of many people through a consideration of policy areas which are not conventionally thought of as 'social' policy. Throughout, the aim has been to show that the component parts of social life do relate to the welfare of individuals and families. In so doing there has been an implicit acceptance of the claim of Peter Townsend that relative poverty consists in not being able to have access to or participate in the goods and services and way of life that the majority of people in the society deem to be important (Townsend, 1979, p. 915). The integrative focus that Titmuss and an earlier generation of social policy writers saw in the institutions of the 'welfare state' was in a society where public services were used by a much greater percentage of the population. This is no longer the case, and many people have chosen private options wherever they can, particularly in transport and housing. What is becoming increasingly clear is that choice is very restricted for the poor and all the other groups who because of age or disability are excluded from participation in the consumer society. It may well be that citizenship will fail to engage with the aspirations of a majority of the population because they prefer the more limited social involvement which consumerism entails. We do not know. The mass consumer society emerged only a few years after the 'welfare state' in Britain and it seems clear that the direction and shape of the welfare state will continue to be related to the decisions that citizens make as consumers. It behoves us, if we want to understand the complexity of Social Policy, to study it in the context of the everyday life of a consumer society.

References

Dunn, M and Smith, S (1990), 'Economic Policy and Privatisation', in S P Savage and L Robins (eds), *Public Policy under Thatcher*, London: Macmillan.

Durning, A T (1992), *How Much is Enough? The Consumer Society and the Future of the Earth*, London: Earthscan.

Easterlin, R (1974), 'Does economic growth improve the human lot?', in P A David and M Reder (eds), *Nations and Households in Economic Growth*, London: Academic Press.

Giddens, A (1991), *Modernity and Identity*, Cambridge: Polity Press.

Golding, P (ed.) (1986), *Excluding the Poor*, London: Child Poverty Action Group.

Gyford, J (1991), *Citizens, Consumers and Councils*, London: Macmillan.

Irvine, S (1989), *Beyond Green Consumerism*, London: Friends of the Earth.

Jacobs, M (1991), *The Green Economy*, London: Pluto Press.

Le Grand, J (1982), *The Strategy of Equality*, London: George Allen and Unwin.

Lunt, P K and Livingstone, S M (1992), *Mass Consumption and Personal Identity*, Buckingham: Open University Press.

Marquand, D (1991), *The Progressive Dilemma*, London: Heinemann.

Marshall, T H (1963), 'Citizenship and Social Class', in *Sociology at the Cross Roads*, London: Heinemann.

Meadows, D H et al. (1972), *The Limits to Growth*, New York: Universe Books.

Moseley, M J (1979), *Accessibility: the rural challenge*, London: Methuen.

Oldfield, A (1990), *Citizenship and Community*, London: Routledge.

Pahl, R E (1984), *Divisions of Labour*, Oxford: Basil Blackwell.

Roche, M (1992), *Rethinking Citizenship*, Cambridge: Polity Press.

Stewart, J (1992), 'Guidelines for public service management: lessons not to be learnt from the private sector', in Pam Carter et al. (eds), *Changing Social Work and Welfare*, London: Open University Press.

Taylor Gooby, P (1991), *Social Change, Social Science and Social Welfare*, Hemel Hempstead: Harvester Wheatsheaf.

Townsend, P (1979), *Poverty in the United Kingdom*, Harmondsworth: Penguin Books.

GLOSSARY

BARCODE vertical lines of different widths which represent a numeric code. Read by light pens.

CABLE TELEVISION television service transmitted along underground cables to the subscriber's home from a booster station. Some cable services now provide a complete telephone service in addition.

CD ROM Compact Disk Read Only Memory. The compact disks used for audio recordings are capable of holding vast quantities of information, approximately 600 million characters. Increasingly used as a data storage form by libraries.

DIGITAL a way of storing data where it is represented as a series of coded pulses with only two possible states: 'on' or 'off'. These signals can be more easily be stored or saved and transmitted than previous methods.

ELECTRONIC MAIL or E-Mail. A system which permits computer users to transmit messages and documents. These messages are stored on the computer at the point of delivery for collection at any time.

FAX or Facsimile transmission. A way of transmitting a copy of an image on paper via the telephone system.

FIBRE OPTICS pulses of light transmitted along optical fibres. These cables can transmit a much greater amount of information than copper cables for longer distances and are less susceptible to electrical interference.

FLOPPY DISK a disk made of flexible plastic that stores computer data.

HARDWARE the manufactured components of a telecommunications system.

HYPERTEXT a way of organizing information which is based on a variety of associations permitting multiple linkages. The information can be text, graphics or video.

INFORMATION TECHNOLOGY electronic technology used for collecting, storing, processing and communicating information. It includes computers and telecommunications.

ISDN Integrated Services Digital Network. Digital networks which transmit voice and data over a single line.

MAINFRAME Mainframe computer. A large centralized system in an organization which is often used for large data processing jobs.

MICROCHIPS or silicon chips. A very small piece of silicon containing an integrated circuit first used on computer but now to be found in a host of industrial and domestic products.

MICROCOMPUTERS a small computer system. Often used to refer to a personal computer but includes bank terminals and games machines.

MODEM Modulator/Demodulator. A device that links a computer to other computers using the telephone line.

ONLINE part of a computer system which is under the control of that system. Online databases permit large amounts of information to be accessed worldwide from terminals.

SATELLITE TELEVISION The use of satellites as relay stations for television channels. Viewers can receive transmissions either with their own satellite dish or via a cable company which provides satellite channels.

SOFTWARE computer programs.

TELECOMMUNICATIONS transmission of information via electronic signals. Includes radio waves, cable and fibre optics.

TELEPORT a building which gives access to telecommunications services.

VIDEOTEXT an information service which is available using a television set. Pages of information are displayed on the screen which users can browse through and then if they wish order goods and services from information providers.

INDEX